Engagement
BY DESIGN

DOUGLAS FISHER • NANCY FREY • RUSSELL J. QUAGLIA
DOMINIQUE SMITH • LISA L. LANDE

Engagement
BY DESIGN

CREATING
LEARNING
ENVIRONMENTS
WHERE
STUDENTS
THRIVE

resources.corwin.com/engagementbydesign

CORWIN
LITERACY

FOR INFORMATION:

Corwin
A SAGE Company
2455 Teller Road
Thousand Oaks, California 91320
(800) 233-9936
www.corwin.com

SAGE Publications Ltd.
1 Oliver's Yard
55 City Road
London EC1Y 1SP
United Kingdom

SAGE Publications India Pvt. Ltd.
B 1/I 1 Mohan Cooperative Industrial Area
Mathura Road, New Delhi 110 044
India

SAGE Publications Asia-Pacific Pte. Ltd.
3 Church Street
#10-04 Samsung Hub
Singapore 049483

Publisher and Senior Program Director: Lisa Luedeke
Editorial Development Manager: Julie Nemer
Editorial Assistant: Nicole Shade
Production Editor: Melanie Birdsall
Copy Editor: Diana Breti
Typesetter: C&M Digitals (P) Ltd.
Proofreader: Tricia Currie-Knight
Indexer: Marilyn Augst
Cover Designer: Rose Storey
Marketing Manager: Rebecca Eaton

Printed in the United States of America

ISBN 978-1-5063-7573-1

This book is printed on acid-free paper.

SUSTAINABLE FORESTRY INITIATIVE
Certified Chain of Custody
Promoting Sustainable Forestry
www.sfiprogram.org
SFI-01268
SFI label applies to text stock

18 19 20 21 10 9 8 7 6 5 4

Contents

online
resources

Visit the companion website at
resources.corwin.com/engagementbydesign
for videos and downloadable resources.

List of Videos

Note From the Publisher: The authors have provided video and web content throughout the book that is available to you through QR (quick response) codes. To read a QR code, you must have a smartphone or tablet with a camera. We recommend that you download a QR code reader app that is made specifically for your phone or tablet brand.

Videos may also be accessed at
resources.corwin.com/engagementbydesign

Acknowledgments

Corwin gratefully acknowledges the contributions of the following reviewers:

Lydia Bowden
Assistant Principal
Pinckneyville Middle School
Peachtree Corners, GA

Lynn Angus Ramos
Language Arts Curriculum Coordinator
DeKalb County School District
Decatur, GA

Melanie Spence
Assistant Principal/Curriculum Coordinator
Sloan-Hendrix School District
Imboden, AR

About the Authors

Douglas Fisher, PhD, is professor of educational leadership at San Diego State University and a teacher-leader at Health Sciences High & Middle College. He is the recipient of an IRA Celebrate Literacy Award, the NCTE's Farmer Award for Excellence in Writing, and a Christa McAuliffe Award for Excellence in Teacher Education. A former board member for the Literacy Research Association and a current board member for the International Literacy Association, Doug is also a credentialed English teacher and administrator in California. Doug can be reached at dfisher@mail.sdsu.edu.

Nancy Frey, PhD, is professor of educational leadership at San Diego State University and a teacher-leader at Health Sciences High & Middle College. A credentialed special educator, reading specialist, and administrator in California, Nancy is also the recipient of both the 2008 Early Career Achievement Award from the Literacy Research Association and a Christa McAuliffe award for Excellence in

Teacher Education from the American Association of State Colleges and Universities. Nancy can be reached at nfrey@mail.sdsu.edu.

Nancy and Doug collaborate often. *Teaching Literacy in the Visible Learning Classroom, K–5* and *6–12* (Corwin Literacy, 2017), *Visible Learning for Literacy* (Corwin Literacy, 2016), *Text Complexity*, 2nd edition (Corwin Literacy, 2016), *Text-Dependent Questions, K–5* and *6–12* (Corwin Literacy, 2014), and *Rigorous Reading* (Corwin Literacy, 2013) are some of the more recent titles among their many best-selling texts.

 **Dr. Russell J. Quaglia** is a globally recognized pioneer in the field of education, known for his unwavering dedication to student voice and aspirations. Russell has been described by news media as America's foremost authority on the development and achievement of student voice and aspirations. His innovative work is evidenced by an extensive library of research-based publications, prominent international speaking appearances, and a successfully growing list of aspirations ventures.

Among these ventures, Russell authored the School Voice suite of surveys, including Student Voice, Teacher Voice, Parent Voice, and iKnow My Class. His recent book, *Student Voice: The Instrument of Change*, published by Corwin, is already receiving international acclaim.

In addition to founding and leading the Quaglia Institute for Student Aspirations, Russell also founded and currently chairs the Aspirations Academies Trust, a sponsor of primary and secondary academies in England built upon his aspirations research. Most recently he has founded the Teacher Voice and Aspirations International Center, dedicated to amplifying the voice of teachers in order for them to realize their aspirations and reach their fullest potential.

Russell earned his bachelor's degree at Assumption College, a master's degree in economics from Boston College, and master of education and doctorate degrees from Columbia University, specializing in the area of organizational theory and behavior. He has been awarded numerous honorary doctorates in humanitarian services for his dedication to students. Russell's work has also led him to serve on several national and international committees, reflecting his passion for ensuring that students' and teachers' voices are always heard, honored, and acted upon.

Dominique Smith is a social worker, school administrator, mentor, national trainer for the International Institute on Restorative Practices, and he is the co-author of *Building Equity: Policies and Practices to Empower All Learners*. He is passionate about creating school cultures that honor students and build their confidence and competence. He is the winner of the National School Safety Award from the School Safety Advocacy Council.

Dr. Lisa L. Lande has dedicated her professional endeavors to advocating for teachers and students around the globe. It is her aspiration that every classroom in every school be one that she would want her own three children to learn in—a lens through which she continually measures her research, writing, and professional development efforts.

She is the executive director of the Teacher Voice and Aspirations International Center (TVAIC), an outgrowth of the Quaglia Institute. The mission of TVAIC is to amplify teacher voice to enhance the aspirations of all. As part of the Quaglia Institute team, Lisa has provided professional development services to PreK–12 schools throughout the United States, Canada, England, and the Middle East.

Lisa currently serves as a board member for the Aspirations Academy Trust in England. She is the co-author of *Teacher Voice: Amplifying Success*.

THE INVITING CLASSROOM

Visitors to Mark Castro's classroom always say the same thing: "The students were so engaged! There were no behavior problems, and they all seemed to be working on complex and interesting tasks." It should go without saying that this does not just happen by chance. Mr. Castro works hard to ensure that the learning environment is conducive for all students' developing knowledge, skills, and dispositions.

Entering Mr. Castro's classroom, visitors typically note the organization of the environment. There are a number of different desk and seating options, from stools to exercise balls to standing tables. They also tend to notice the environmental print; the walls are rich with information that the class has obviously created together. When they finally look down, visitors often notice that students sit in groups and are usually involved in different tasks. Some groups have laptops and iPads on their tables, while others have printed texts. Visitors often ask Mr. Castro whether he has an electronic device for every student. His response is instructive. He says, "Yes, I do, but I don't have students using the devices at the same time. Doing so encourages more individual, independent work, and I want to make sure that my students have lots of opportunities to talk with their peers as they wrestle with the learning expectations. In fact, it's rare for me to have all of the technology out at once. The last time I did was for state testing, last spring."

Visitors also notice the range of interactions students have within the classroom. Some groups are engaged in animated discussions, and others are sitting knee to knee, talking with a partner. At one table, a group of students is discussing the questions that they want to ask another group.

"I think that we should first ask about the big idea," Andrew says, *"Like why the author wrote this."*

Tierra agrees. *"I like that because I don't think we should just start with the details because then it gets too boring to just find the information that's right there."*

"But I do think we should have some detail questions ready because there are some important things to remember, but they can come after the big ideas,"

Brianna adds. *"Remember, we're supposed to be making sure that they understood this [pointing to the paper]. Who knows how we will be asked to show that we understand? So I think we need to make sure that details are included."*

Andrew responds, *"Good point. Can we each write one question and then ask each other the questions so that we can test them out and talk about them?"*

The group gets to work.

Mr. Castro walks around the room, stopping in to meet with various groups of students as they complete learning tasks. Periodically, Mr. Castro interrupts the activity and draws students' attention.

During one lesson, he said, *"I think we might have found a really cool error. Let's talk through this to see if it's an error because, if it is, we can all learn from it."* Mr. Castro continues, explaining the response from a student and allowing the class to discuss the response and where thinking might have gone astray. Visitors often note the framed poster that reads, "We celebrate errors as opportunities to learn." ☝

Visitors are never surprised to learn that Mr. Castro's students perform exceptionally well on the state achievement tests. But they are surprised to learn that all of his students are at risk for educational failure in one way or another. They all live in poverty, and many have attended multiple schools. Several students are learning English as an additional language, and five of his 33 students have identified disabilities. When asked about his students' achievement, Mr. Castro is humble and simply says, "My students want to learn. They just need to be shown the way." In a large part, Mr. Castro's students achieve because they are engaged in learning.

Are Students Engaged?

Have you ever had someone visit your classroom and say something like, "Four students were not engaged"? Or perhaps you were the one who said that. What evidence is used to make that statement? Most likely the statement was based on behavioral engagement rather than cognitive engagement. To us, there is a significant difference between

Video 1
What Is Engagement?

resources.corwin.com/
engagementbydesign

To read a QR code, you must have a smartphone or tablet with a camera. We recommend that you download a QR code reader app that is made specifically for your phone or tablet brand.

Behavioral vs Cognitive Engagement

behavioral and cognitive engagement. Behavioral engagement is easy to observe. Typically, we think students are engaged if they track the speaker with their eyes, sit up in the chair, and generally look like they are paying attention. In general, we call these actions "teacher-pleasing behaviors" because they do just that, make teachers (and administrators) happy. But they don't necessarily mean that students are learning.

Consider two students in the same class. Brandon sits next to the window and always seems more interested in the events that occur outside. If you came to the classroom, you might say that Brandon was not engaged in learning. However, if you talked with Brandon, he could tell you everything that was said, as well as all of the happenings with squirrels and people outside. Two rows over from Brandon is Heber. Heber tracks the teacher as she speaks, holds a pencil as if ready to write at any second, and sits still in his chair. However, if you asked Heber what the lesson was about, he would probably not be able to tell you. Of course, there are other students in the class for whom there is a better match between their behavioral and cognitive engagement, but it can be hard to tell the difference between the two.

A few years ago, we were interested in the impact that teacher-pleasing behaviors could have on teachers' perceptions and students' learning. We taught one teacher-pleasing behavior to a group of 36 students each week. They happened to be ninth graders, and their other teachers did not know that we were focused on these behaviors. One week we had them greet their teachers upon entering the classroom. For the next couple of weeks, we focused on SLANT:

S = Sit up straight in the chair

L = Lean forward toward the teacher

A = Act interested

N = Nod and smile occasionally

T = Track the teacher with your eyes

In the weeks following SLANT, we had them make physical contact with their teachers (handshake, fist bump, high five, etc.). Then, we asked them to keep their notebooks open on the table and to hold a pen or pencil at all times. We continued, teaching students to ask relevant questions, praise the teacher, and to provide cues or redirections for other students in the class. By the end of the semester, the 34 students (two transferred out) had statistically higher grade point averages than all other ninth graders. And their citizenship grades were incredible: All of them had earned "excellent" or "very good" on their citizenship grades.

We tell this story to highlight that there can be a positive relationship between behavioral engagement, cognitive engagement, and learning. — 3 separate
If you think about it, when this group of students engaged in teacher-pleasing behaviors, their grades probably increased because the teachers noticed them a bit more. But then, their grades probably increased because they were actually paying more attention to the class and were actually learning the content better. Yes, behavioral engagement is important, but we also worry about students like Heber whose behavioral engagement masks his cognitive disengagement.

That's why monitoring cognitive engagement is essential. It is easier to tell whether students are cognitively engaged when the classroom is filled with discussion and dialogue. As students interact with each other and their teachers, their thinking becomes evident. It is public and available for others to respond to. It becomes fodder for future lessons and interactions that continue to shape students' understanding of the world. In other words, discussion and dialogue provide students and their teachers with evidence of cognitive engagement and of learning.

That was the long way around to say that engagement is our goal, both cognitively and behaviorally. In fact, we believe that engagement in learning is one of the major contributors to student achievement. Said another way, it's hard for students to learn when they're not engaged. To nerd out a bit, there is considerable neuroscience that confirms this point. Here's the chain reaction. For learning to occur, the student has to engage in selective attention, which means that the student is selecting specific information and inputs over all other possibilities. To make this more concrete, to learn how to spell the word *surreptitious*, the student would first have to attend to the lesson (or letters, if studying alone) and not the train horn in the distance, the sound of a new text message, the desire to know the score of the game, the feeling of dread at failing, or any of thousands of possible other stimuli.

From selective attention, the student has to move to sustained attention, focusing long enough to process information. This involves working memory and storage functions that are very complicated. The student will also need to make connections between the new information, in this case the spelling of *surreptitious,* and previously known information. To remember the information and to be able to use the information, the student will need practice and rehearsal, all while still paying attention. Taken together, this process is what we mean when we say that a student cognitively engages. To pay attention, to engage working memory, to practice and rehearse, and to use information requires that students engage, and they are more likely to do so in classrooms that are inviting.

Intentionally Inviting Classrooms

Although school is compulsory, learning is not. The act of learning is analogous to a dance between teacher and learner. However, an unwilling dance partner upsets the equation. You may think we're referring to the learner, but actually we mean the teacher. Much like the lead dance partner, the teacher guides the student through the choreography. The best leads convey a sense of invitation throughout, through missteps and moments of fluidity. *I've got you. We're in this together.* But the teacher who doesn't attend to the invitational elements risks a reduced impact on learning. This effect snowballs, as the teacher who doesn't get results begins to experience a decline in self-efficacy. *I just don't have good dance partners*, the thinking goes. *If I had better dancers, I'd get better results.*

An invitational stance to learning is key to getting results. Purkey and Novak (1996) describe invitational education through four lenses. The first is *trust*, which describes the ongoing relationships between the teacher and students. In trusting classrooms, teachers and students assume positive intentions and seek to build, maintain, and repair those

---

An invitational stance to learning is key to getting results.

Video 2
The Intentionally
Inviting Classroom

*resources.corwin.com/
engagementbydesign*

relationships. In other words, trust involves the shared investment we place in other human beings. Trust is a mediating factor
in group cohesion, academic risk-taking, satisfaction, and problem resolution. It forms the bedrock of any high-functioning
classroom.

> **Elements of Invitational Education**
>
> 1. Trust
> 2. Respect
> 3. Optimism
> 4. Intentionality

The second element of invitational education is *respect*. This condition is fostered through actions that communicate an understanding of everyone's autonomy, identity, and value to the
learning community.

2) Respect

Shared responsibility is crucial, and members of the classroom, including the teacher, see themselves as stewards for maintaining the social
and emotional well-being of others.

Optimism is the third element in Purkey and Novak's (1996) construct *3.) optimism*
and arguably our favorite. The assumption is that the potential of each
classroom member is untapped and that every member of the classroom
is responsible for finding ways to help others reach their potential.
Teachers are important in creating optimistic learning environments,
and so are students. In an inviting classroom, students support the
learning of their peers and understand that they are key in others' learning. Purkey and Novak believe that a life without hope impairs a person's ability to move forward. If schools are not places to find hope, then
what use are they?

That leads us to the fourth element: *intentionality*. An invitation to  *4.) Intentionality*
learning means that the practices, policies, processes, and programs of
classrooms and schools are carefully designed to convey trust, respect,
and optimism to all. And by *all*, we mean students, staff, and community members. But what we say we do and what *happens in reality*
can be two different things, thereby undermining a hope-filled school.
Intentionality is, well, intentional.

Teachers can choose to be intentional or not. And they can also be
inviting or not. Purkey and Novak (1996) noted that these two options
resulted in four different types of teachers (see Figure 1.1).

FOUR TYPES OF TEACHERS

Intentionally uninviting teachers . . .	Intentionally inviting teachers . . .
• Are judgmental and belittling • Display little care or regard • Are uninterested in the lives and feelings of students • Isolate themselves from school life • Seek power over students	• Are consistent and steady with students • Notice learning and struggle • Respond regularly with feedback • Seek to build, maintain, and repair relationships
Unintentionally uninviting teachers . . .	Unintentionally inviting teachers . . .
• Distance themselves from students • Have low expectations • Don't feel effective and blame students for shortcomings • Fail to notice student learning or struggle • Offer little feedback to learners	• Are eager but unreflective • Are energetic but rigid when facing problems • Are unaware of what works in their practice and why • Have fewer means for responding when student learning is resistant to their usual methods

Figure 1.1

- **Intentionally uninviting teachers,** although thankfully rare, can leave an indelible mark on a person. Nancy still shudders when she recalls her sixth-grade teacher, who gave demeaning nicknames to students, including one the teacher called "Funeral," because "your face looks like you just came from one." Such teachers are harsh and vindictive and have no place in any school. The one bright spot is that school leaders did their jobs, and this was the only year the woman taught in Nancy's school.

- **Unintentionally uninviting teachers** are, unfortunately, more common. These teachers hold low expectations of their students, which is often the product of disillusionment and a damaged sense of self-efficacy. They blame students and their circumstances when learning stalls. It's not that they dislike children—in fact, it's often just the opposite. But they don't perceive why students don't like their classes or respond enthusiastically to their teaching. Beyond the damage they do at the classroom level, they undermine school improvement efforts by responding negatively and pessimistically. *That will never work with* these *kids*, they say. School leaders often work around these folks rather than with them, unfortunately deepening their diminished sense of efficacy.

- **Unintentionally inviting teachers** are full of enthusiasm for what they do and the students they teach, but they lack the ability to reflect on their practices. Although they may be successful with most students, they don't have the capacity to dig deeper when they encounter a hard-to-reach student. That's because they haven't explored what is working and why. Don't believe the axiom that teachers are born, not made. Unintentionally inviting teachers operate under this misconception. In time, and after too many failures, they become unintentionally disinviting teachers, who also lack the self-perception to analyze successes and challenges.

- **Intentionally inviting teachers** know that becoming a great teacher is purposeful, and they believe that continuous improvement is key. They are consistent and reliable and embody a growth mindset about themselves and their students. Most important, they are perceptive about their students at an individual level, and they know their students well because they invest daily in relationship building. At its best, an invitational classroom permeates the entire milieu, including classroom procedures, the physical environment, and the relationships between teacher, student, and content. Intentionally inviting teachers understand that "*everybody* and *everything* adds to, or subtracts from, connecting with students," and they strive to constantly interrogate their practices (Purkey, 1991, p. 7).

We hope that all classrooms are intentionally inviting places in which students learn. To our thinking, there are easier and harder places to start

Don't believe the axiom that teachers are born, not made.

Video 3
The Intentionally Inviting Teacher

resources.corwin.com/
engagementbydesign

to change a classroom (or school) that is something other than intentionally inviting. We recommend starting with the low-hanging fruit.

Low-Hanging Fruit

The *Urban Dictionary* defines *low-hanging fruit* as "targets or goals which
are easily achievable and which do not require a lot of effort" (http://
www.urbandictionary.com). In our search for what works best, we've
discovered that some of the research-based solutions are time consuming, expensive, or impractical. For example, some have argued that 1:1
computer initiatives are an answer to student engagement issues (see
Harper & Milman, 2016, for a 10-year review). To implement a 1:1 initiative, the district has to have a lot of money and a lot of capacity to
ensure implementation. Just look at the efforts of Los Angeles Unified
School District. Their well-meaning technology effort failed to realize
gains and, in many places in the district, was never even implemented.

Some evidence-based solutions seem to work in the proverbial lab, but
they have never been tried in actual classrooms, which are complex and
diverse. For example, the theory of matching students' learning styles
with classroom instruction is appealing and has a surface logic to it.
It seems reasonable to suggest that students whose preferred learning
style is visual-spatial could achieve more if taught that way. But the
theory doesn't really work out in actual classroom implementation. In
fact, there is no compelling evidence that matching learning style with
instruction will accelerate achievement.

Having said that, it's important to note that there are also research-
based recommendations that seem quite reasonable to implement.
They are understandable, they translate well into classroom practice,
they are not too expensive, and they don't require extensive professional learning to implement. For us, that's the low-hanging fruit that
we are interested in. And to extend the metaphor even further, once
the low-hanging fruit has been harvested, then we can pay attention
to high-hanging fruit. After all, why go after the hardest to implement
school improvement effort when there are easier to implement tools
that have not been tried?

One of the places we, and millions of other people, go to for inspiration on what to implement next is John Hattie's (2009) seminal review of educational research. Hattie has synthesized thousands of research studies and calculated effect sizes to determine which influences have a strong likelihood of success in terms of students' learning. Effect size is a statistical tool used to determine the average impact of a specific influence or action. Hattie was able to scale these various influences to determine which of them worked best. As Hattie noted, 95% of what teachers do works, if they expect zero growth for the year. Yes, you read that right. If you do not expect any growth, then teachers and schools do little harm. But we should expect students to grow at least a year for each year that they are in school. And some students need to grow a lot more to catch up to where they should be. Thus, it seems reasonable that we should focus on influences, strategies, and actions that have a chance of ensuring that students learn at least a year for each year that they are in school. According to Hattie, an effect size of 0.40 equals one year of learning for one year of school. Thus, we should generally focus on actions that exceed an effect size of 0.40.

> Only 38% of students report that their classes help them understand what is happening in their everyday lives.

But which ones should be tried first? Hattie has calculated effect sizes for nearly 200 influences on students' learning. We wondered, *Where is the low-hanging fruit?* What combination of these influences could be useful in ensuring that students learn? How could this seemingly random collection of influences be organized in such a way that teachers, teams, and entire school systems could get started on improving the experiences students have?

Student Voice

In addition to citing the seminal work of John Hattie (2009) and other researchers with insights to offer on the topic of engagement, we will be drawing heavily on the voices of students themselves, as one of our core beliefs is that students have something to teach us. Throughout this book, we will reference current results from the Quaglia Student Voice Survey. A total of 48,185 students in Grades 6 to 12 and 12,157 students in Grades 3 to 5 took the Student Voice Survey during the 2015–2016 school year, representing 249 schools across 14 states. Underpinning data results from the Student Voice Survey are three primary goals:

1. Share what we are learning from the voices of students

2. Present data in a manner that is understandable rather than overwhelming, and provide a useful context

3. Provide valuable suggestions and next steps that demonstrate how the information gleaned from the Student Voice Survey can have an immediate impact in schools

Only 52% of students report that their teachers make an effort to get to know them, and only 43% believe teachers care about their problems and feelings.

For a full account of these survey results, see the 2016 National School Voice Report, which can be downloaded for free at www.quagliainstitute.org.

We cannot assume that because kids talk the student voice is present, and it is important that we do not confuse voice with complaints or challenging authority. When we work to develop skills to effectively utilize their voice, we focus on three things designed to support students (and adults!):

*   **Listening.** Listening more than trying to convince others to agree with their existing perspectives

*   **Learning.** Making an intentional and authentic effort to learn from what they hear when listening

*   **Leading.** Taking responsibility to lead with others in taking actions that will make the world a better place (Quaglia, 2016)

Why are we so passionate about amplifying student voice? Not only because we think it is the right thing to do, but also because impact analysis studies have shown us that when students have a voice in school, they are seven times more likely to be academically motivated. That is something worth working for!

Engagement by Design

As we have noted, if learners fail to pay attention, engage, and use their voice in a meaningful way, they're not likely to learn. It seems obvious,

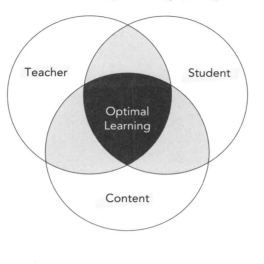

Figure 1.2

but too often we see classrooms where teachers are "teaching" (or at least telling) but no one is paying any attention. Students pay attention when the lesson is engaging, but we use the word *engaging* differently from some others. We aim for cognitive engagement, which is much harder to monitor. Cognitive engagement—and thus optimal learning—comes from the intersection of the teacher, the student, and the content (see, e.g., City, Elmore, Fiarman, & Tietel, 2009). We like to think of this in terms of overlapping circles that provide a balanced approach to the learning experience (see Figure 1.2).

Take the overlap of the student and the teacher. The amount of overlap between those two theoretical circles is a relationship (see Figure 1.3). And yes, relationships are important and impact student learning. In fact, Hattie (2009) found that teacher-student relationships have an effect size of 0.72. Yet only 52% of students report that their teachers make an effort to get to know them, and only 43% believe teachers care about their problems and feelings. Clearly, some people do not yet understand the value of relationships. In fact, Doug remembers his well-meaning supervisor from his first year whose advice was, "Don't

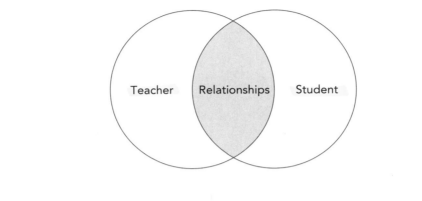

Figure 1.3

smile until winter break." Doug took the advice and avoided asking students questions about their interests and didn't tell them anything about his passions. Needless to say, Doug's students didn't learn much that year. It was terrible advice. Instead, Doug's advisor should have said, "Do all you can to develop strong, productive, growth-producing relationships with students." And parenthetically, positive teacher-student relationships are low-hanging fruit. Teachers can choose their attitudes toward students and can purposefully work to develop positive relationships. That's why we think of this as one piece of low-hanging fruit.

Let's take another overlapping set of circles, this time between the teacher and the content (see Figure 1.4). We think of this overlap as teacher clarity. Teachers should know their content. They should not be teaching incorrect information or missing critical aspects of the content. They should also let students know *what* they are supposed to be learning and *why*. However, only 38% of students report that their classes help them understand what is happening in their everyday lives. Further, teachers and students should understand what

CLARITY

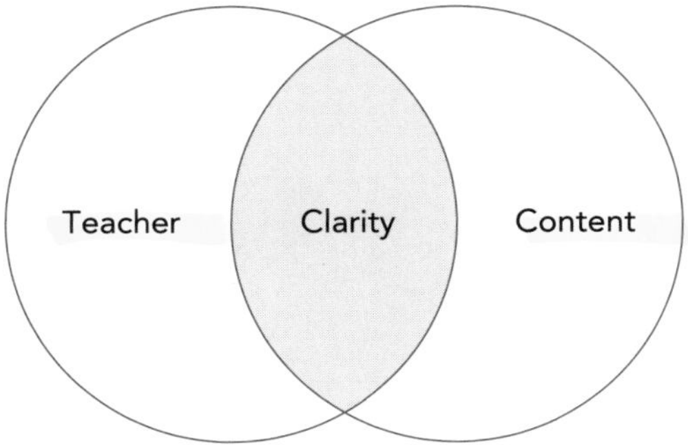

Teacher   Clarity   Content

Figure 1.4

success looks like. Teacher clarity—the combination of teachers knowing what they are supposed to be teaching, informing students about what they are supposed to be learning, and reaching agreements with students about the success criteria—has a strong impact on students' learning. According to Hattie (2009), the effect size of teacher clarity is 0.75. Really, it's not that hard to figure out what students need to learn. It requires an understanding of the standards and a willingness to identify what students already know. It's also not hard to inform students about the daily learning intentions, nor is it hard to identify what success looks like. Teacher clarity is another piece of low-hanging fruit that is all too often left on the learning tree, ignored by otherwise well-intentioned teachers.

The third possible overlapping circles are formed by considering the student and the content (see Figure 1.5). The amount of overlap between these two is known as challenge. Students appreciate a worthy challenge. According to Hattie (2009), a high level of challenge has an effect size of 0.57. Students are not interested in low-level, boring lessons, and 43% of students report that currently, school *is* boring! They

Teacher clarity— teachers knowing what they are supposed to be teaching, informing students about what they are supposed to be learning, and negotiating success criteria with students.

CHALLENGE

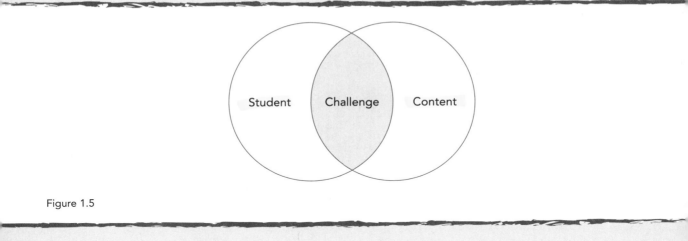

Figure 1.5

expect school to be a challenge, and they welcome the opportunity to rise to the challenge. Seventy-three percent of students tell us they put forth their best effort, and 85% say getting good grades is important to them. Of course, a high level of challenge requires that teachers create appropriate tasks and that they hold high expectations for students. Again, challenge is a low-hanging fruit and one that is easily within the reach of the teacher.

But what happens when we put all three of these circles together? If we overlap the student circle with the content circle and the teacher circle, there is a place where they all touch, and that is engagement.

Students engage when they have relationships with teachers who know their content and who make sure learning is relevant, interesting, and challenging. The experiences that teachers plan need to take into account each of these. Downloading a lesson from the Internet may help with planning, but it may not be responsive to a given group of students. There is no perfect lesson plan, and there is no one right way to teach content. Teachers are always designing and adjusting their lessons based on the students in their classes.

Conclusion

Effective classrooms don't just happen. They are led by teachers who deeply understand their craft and the essential nature of the interaction between student, teacher, and content. These teachers strive to be intentionally inviting, in that they build and monitor the ways in which their classroom practices, policies, processes, and programs align to send a welcoming and supportive message. You've undoubtedly set foot in these places before; perhaps your own classroom is a model of invitation. In the chapters that follow, we will further explore the nature of relationships, clarity, and challenge to optimize engagement. And as with any invitation, it begins with a welcoming message.

73% of students say they put forth their best effort, and 85% say getting good grades is important to them.

RELATIONSHIPS

© Bill Aron/PhotoEdit

Hector says that he was a "terror" in middle school. He was gang affiliated and stole from other students to support his drug habit. He was often suspended for defiant behaviors. He was eventually expelled for punching the principal during an altercation. Hector was then enrolled in a continuation school, where he says that he learned a lot of new skills, including how to deal drugs and carry a weapon. He was expelled from the continuation school when he was caught with a large amount of money and marijuana, selling to other students. When asked, Hector says, "In sixth grade, no one knew my name. No teacher ever called me by my name and we just called them 'teacher' or 'Mr.' when we wanted them. I can't remember any of them, really. When I started to get into trouble, they all knew my name but only said it when I was in trouble. I never really knew those teachers, and I didn't care about them. Really, they were just in my way most of the time."

At the start of high school, Hector enrolled in a new school. Actually, his mother enrolled him in a new school in a new district, hoping that his past would not follow him. Hector refused to acknowledge his teachers and said to one of them, on the second day of school, "You don't have the right to look me in the eye."

By the end of the first week of school, Hector had made himself known to the faculty. On the first Friday of the school year, at their first professional learning event of the year, teachers identified students who needed extra help or attention. Every one of Hector's teachers wrote his name on an index card. Once all of the cards were sorted to identify duplicates, they were shuffled and then distributed to staff. Each staff member—teachers, paraprofessionals, office and support, maintenance and custodial—received a card. The cards were to be passed around until they were gone. Some staff members had two cards; others had three.

The following week, the adult who received the card would find the student and start a conversation, as long as it was nothing about school. This would continue, daily, until a strong relationship was built. The staff was trying to establish trusting relationships with high-risk students using the **two by ten strategy** (Ginsberg & Wlodkowski, 2004), in which the staff member has a two-minute conversation with student for 10 consecutive days, talking nothing about school or work. Once the 10 consecutive days have passed, the two individuals can talk about anything else they want, including school performance. At that time, the staff member also attempts to broker better relationships between the student and other adults in that student's life. At the same time, the other adults in that student's life are also trying to develop strong relationships with all of their other students.

Returning to Hector, it took nine weeks before David Samuels was able to talk with him for 10 consecutive days. At first, Hector used a lot of curse words. He walked out of class whenever he wanted. He refused to shake hands with Mr. Samuels or anyone else at school. The first quarter of the year was rough, but each time he transgressed, someone at the school would talk with him about the harm that was being done.

On reflection, Hector said, "I really thought that they were all soft. I mean, they never really got me in trouble. It was kinda annoying to talk all of the time, but I was like, okay, so I talk with them, and then I get to go back to class or whatever. But really, I started to be less bad because they noticed me. I still had a reputation, so I did stupid stuff, but it wasn't as bad as before, mostly because they seemed to care so much."

By the end of November, Hector and Mr. Samuels had a reasonably strong relationship. They shook hands every time they saw each other, and Hector regularly sought out Mr. Samuels to tell him things that were happening in his life. Hector still did not have a great relationship with any of his teachers, but they noted a slight improvement in his behavior. Then, the first week of December, Hector got really angry during English. He yelled in class, threw his books on the floor, cursed, and stormed out of the classroom. His English teacher, Andrea Salazar, messaged the principal, who went to find Hector. Hector was outside the bathroom, clearly very upset. His hands were balled into fists and his eyes were red, and it looked like he could cry.

Acknowledging the principal with his eyes, he choked out, "Can you get Mr. Samuels?" which she did.

The principal found coverage for Mr. Samuels and he went to talk with Hector. When Hector saw Mr. Samuels, he started crying. He said,

"Man, I tried so hard, but it ain't worth it. They think I'm stupid. I can't get the words right on the vocab, and they make fun of me."

Mr. Samuels asked who made fun of him, and Hector responded, "I ain't no snitch. I just want outta here."

Mr. Samuels responded, "Can you at least tell me if it was an adult or a student?" to which Hector responded, "Students."

Mr. Samuels walked Hector to the office and invited him to stay in the office as long as he needed for the rest of the period. Before leaving, Mr. Samuels said, "Later today, maybe at the first part of lunch, can we talk with Ms. Salazar so she knows what's going on?" Hector agreed.

During that conversation, Ms. Salazar was able to tell Hector that she was scared by his behavior and also worried about his education. Over the course of the conversation, Hector and Ms. Salazar became a bit closer, and she became one of his advocates and allies. This proved to be another turning point. By the end of the first semester, Hector routinely shook hands with his teachers, called them by name, and was generally pleasant in class. His ninth-grade year still had a number of ups and downs, like the situation with the vocabulary test, but Hector was slowly becoming more trusting of the adults in his school and his behavior was evening out much more.

Fast-forward a few years, and Hector was well known by all of the staff of the school. He excelled in his internship and rarely was angry at school anymore. He informed Mr. Samuels that he was "clean for five months now" and that he took a drug test at home (by his choice) to show his mom. During a parent conference, his mom said, "What did you do to him? He's totally different now. He helps me in the house and talks nicer to me. He still goes out, sometimes too late, but then he says sorry to me and doesn't do that for a while."

During his senior year, Hector studied with Mr. Samuels for the Armed Services Vocational Aptitude Battery (ASVAB) test so that he could join the Army, which he did immediately following graduation. Mr. Samuels flew to Texas to participate in his graduation from boot camp because Hector's mom was not able to travel due to immigration issues. At graduation,

Hector said, "Tell the teachers thank you. I wouldn't be here right now if they didn't believe in me and take the time to get to know me. I was a bad kid, but I had a good heart, and you all found it."

That was a fairly long story to make a simple point: relationships matter. Strong teacher-student relationships can change lives. But it doesn't have to be that dramatic. Healthy teacher-student relationships remove a lot of learning barriers for students, allowing them to feel safe enough to focus on the lessons presented to them. According to the national Student Voice data, only 67% of students feel accepted for who they are at school, and without feeling accepted or safe, it is impossible to give their full attention to learning. As we noted in the previous chapter, it's not just that we think that teachers should focus on relationships because it feels good to do so. There is solid research that relationships positively impact students' learning. For example, Cornelius-White (2007) reviewed 119 studies on teacher-student relationships that included more than 350,000 students and noted, "Positive relationships, non-directivity, empathy, warmth, and encouraging thinking and learning are the specific teacher variables that are above average compared with other educational innovations" (p. 134). Importantly, Cornelius-White noted that there were no differences in the impact that teacher-student relationships had when race/ethnicity differed between the students and their teachers. Simply said, relationships matter.

> # Only 67% of students feel accepted for who they are at school.

Building Relationships With Students

Engagement by design requires explicit and intentional cultivation of relationships with students. What, then, is a healthy, productive teacher-student relationship? To answer that question, we considered the general psychology research on relationships, which suggests that there are four general conditions required (see Figure 2.1):

1. Respect

2. Honesty

3. Trust

4. Communication

Video 4
The Importance
of Relationships

resources.corwin.com/
engagementbydesign

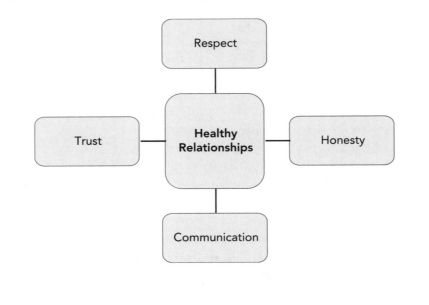

Figure 2.1

Each of these plays an important part in all of the relationships we have with other human beings, whether they are 5, 15, or 55. Having said that, we acknowledge that the teacher-student relationship is a special and unique one. We're not suggesting that teachers become "friends" with students. That is an all-too-common misinterpretation of the research-based recommendations. Friendships require a level of equality, yet there is always a power dynamic between teachers and students. Teachers should be friendly but also maintain the role of the mentor, guide, advocate, and leader.

Connections and Communication

Teacher-student relationships influence our ability to communicate our normative expectations for classroom interactions. To label these expectations "classroom management" minimizes their lasting value.

This is how we mentor the development of young people. The teacher-student relationship is complicated by the very role the teacher plays. At its core, there is an adult-child/youth dynamic that demands developmentally appropriate interactions that are emotionally and psychologically nurturing. For example, adults adjust their language to meet the changing needs of children as they grow and develop. The language used by a kindergarten teacher is different from that of a sixth-grade teacher, but the aim is not. The former may say, *"We are going to practice taking turns. It's not considered polite to interrupt another person who is speaking, so we are going to practice this. And while we wait for our turn, we listen carefully to what the person is saying."* The latter may say, *"I was observing our group interactions and I think I noticed some distractions. Remember we have a goal of tracking the speaker. That means we're looking at the person who is talking and paying attention to that person while he or she speaks."* In both cases, the teacher established an expectation for group interaction but adjusted the language to meet the needs of the specific students. Also, in both cases, the teachers made sure that the children and young adolescents felt secure in their learning and in their status with the adult. In other words, no one was in trouble for not previously engaging in listening to others. That's where "warm and friendly" comes into play.

An Expectation for Learning

Another dynamic in the teacher-student relationship is the expectation for learning. Teachers enter these relationships because they hope to impact the cognitive and behavioral performance of others. In fact, the relationship is founded on the idea that there will be learning. Without this focus, there really is no reason for the significant amount of time that teachers and students spend together. More than a quarter (27%) of students don't think their teachers expect them to be successful. This is something that must change.

Importantly, we know that there is more to learning than academic achievement. Students learn citizenship behaviors,

> More than a quarter (27%) of students don't think their teachers expect them to be successful.

social responsibility, empathy, and a host of other life skills from their teachers. But whatever it is that students and teachers are learning, the fact remains that the relationship is based on an expectation that feedback will be provided such that growth and development can occur. We can't imagine that a single reader of this book would argue against the importance of teacher-student relationships. It's how to develop and maintain them that become the sticking points. To untangle this, we have divided teacher-student relationships into three components:

1. **Invitational.** As part of the relationship, the teacher creates a space that invites students, both psychologically and physically, into learning

2. **Equitable.** As part of the relationship, the teacher ensures that all students have a chance to develop a meaningful relationship with each other and the teacher

3. **Advocacy.** As part of the relationship, the teacher advocates for all members of the classroom community and creates an emotionally safe space for students that is humane and growth-producing, including when relationships have been violated

The Invitational Aspect of Teacher-Student Relationships

Consider times when you have felt welcomed into a new place, such as a neighborhood event. It's likely that people used your name or made a point of learning it. They made sure you had a comfortable place to occupy, and the place looked like they had expected you. Chances are that people took the time to talk with you and to find out more about who you are as a person. These early interactions gave you a sense of belonging. Classrooms shouldn't be any different, and yet only 64% find school to be a welcoming and friendly place. As hosts of the classroom, it is up to teachers to issue the invitation to learn. From there, students will assume responsibility and issue each other invitations to learn. There are several things that teachers can do to signal that students are welcomed and valued.

> Only 64% of students find school to be a welcoming and friendly place.

Learn Their Names

One simple point is to know every student's name, and shockingly, only 52% of students believe their teachers know their name! As humans, we all attach a great deal of importance to our names, and we appreciate when others use them in greetings or conversations. This can be a challenging task, especially for secondary teachers who teach 150–200 students a day. But children and adolescents appreciate our commitment to learning and recalling their names. There are a variety of ways to learn them, from activities such as decorating name tents to be placed on desks, to returning papers and assignments to each student to strengthen the association between name and face. One of our colleagues has his students sit in a circle on the first day of class, asking each person to introduce themselves to the group and then identifying the marine animal that shares a characteristic with him or her ("My name is Ana, and I am like a clownfish because I am colorful and like to make people laugh"). Each subsequent member of the circle then must identify previous classmates by name and marine animal before sharing their own information. The repetition helps, and it prompts everyone to listen closely. Watch for the first glimpses of community building, as classmates silently prompt those who are having difficulty. These early interactions contribute to swift trust, as newly formed teams strive for cohesiveness and shared goals (Ennen, Stark, & Lassiter, 2015; Meyerson, Weick, & Kramer, 1996).

> Shockingly, only 52% of students believe their teachers know their name.

Learn About Their Names

What's the story behind your name? Were you named for an ancestor? Perhaps your name evokes a place or suggests a character trait. Is your name a traditional one that reflects your cultural heritage, or did your parents invent a new name just for you? Ask someone how they got their name, and you're likely to hear a story that is funny, or touching, or downright confounding. Dominique, for example, was named after a basketball player his Fijian father admired. Dominique tells people who ask about his name that most people think his name is feminine and address e-mails to Ms. Smith, or they pronounce it Dominic, because that is what they are used to.

Once students know each other reasonably well, teachers can invite students to learn more about their name by asking family members, conducting Internet research, or finding characters in books with the same name. The fifth graders in Monica Greene's classroom engaged in a study of their names as part of a research and writing unit that involved their family history. Their essays had several parts, including the origin of their names and the personal history of the family. In addition, they had to profile someone in their family and provide more extensive information about that person. Ms. Greene's major academic goal was informational writing, but she decided to focus on students' personal histories and their names so that she could get to know her students better.

Mario didn't know much about his name, but he ended up being very proud of himself based on what he learned. Mario interviewed his grandfather, his mother, and his aunt to piece together his family history project. As part of his paper, Mario wrote the following:

> There are two main reasons why I am named Mario. The first is embarrassing. My dad is Japanese and loves the game Super Mario. In the game, Mario is very powerful and can jump and smash things. My grandfather said that he told my parents that if I was named Mario, I might be able to gain powers from things around me. My grandfather is from the old country and believes in things like that. My aunt said Mario was a good name because he's the good guy in the game. When I talked to her, she said that she hopes that the name helps me stay on a good path. But my mom said that she said yes to Mario because her great uncle's middle name was Mario and he fought for people's rights, like the rights of workers in the fields. All of these reasons make me proud to be Mario and want to be a good person and earn the name.

For additional ideas about name activities, please visit www.ultimate camp resource.com/site/camp-activities/name-games.page-1.html.

Create a Welcoming Space

The way that the classroom is organized also communicates a great deal about who and what is valued. Not too long ago, we visited a classroom that seemed to have a lot of space devoted to the teacher. To verify this, we counted floor tiles and, sure enough, just over one-third of the classroom was "off limits" to students and was used exclusively by the teacher. As one of the students said as we approached the teacher's desk, "She might get mad if you go over there. That's her space." Although it is reasonable for teachers to have storage areas that are reserved for their use, it is wise to consider the ways in which this is explained to students and how much space is not available for learning.

In some classrooms, such as the one profiled in Chapter 1, the teacher has thought creatively about the organization of learning spaces. In Bradley Hanson's science class, there are two types of tables and chairs and the students rotate between them for different activities. At the lower tables and chairs, students take notes, work with technology, or write. At the higher tables, students engage in more collaborative learning and lab work. As Mr. Hanson notes, "The students know what is expected of them based on where they are sitting. We have agreements in this classroom about the type of work that we need to do and where it is most appropriate to complete that work. The room helps to facilitate students' learning because it is their space and they know what to do with it."

In many classrooms, the walls are also used to convey a welcoming environment. Often, this includes student-generated materials that are evidence of their learning. For example, in Kristen Heller's first-grade classroom, students create language charts for each of the books they read. They understand the purpose for the reading and direct their teacher about what to record. While reading *Waiting Is Not Easy* (Willems, 2014), the students wanted to record the names of the characters (Elephant and Piggie) and their characteristics, namely that one is patient and the other is in a hurry. They also wanted to note that Gerald the elephant keeps guessing at the surprise but he's always wrong and that complaining doesn't really help. Once they had talked about the book for a bit, they agreed that the main message was "Good things can happen if you are willing to wait for them," which they asked the teacher to write on the language chart as well. The point of the language chart, or any other student-generated content placed on the walls, is not only to serve as a record of learning but also to reinforce that the room belongs to everyone.

Notice Students Without Strong Relationships

Some schools have systems in place to notice when students have not developed strong relationships with adults, but with 22% of students telling us they have difficulty fitting in at school, we know there is room for improvement. There are a number of ways to do this, but we are fond of the dot activity. On large pieces of chart paper, each student's name is printed. We usually do this on a printer and then tape it to the chart paper. During a teacher professional learning session, whether grade level, department, or whole school, teachers put dots next to the names of students that they have strong relationships with. When everyone has finished placing their dots on the chart paper, the team looks for gaps. Which students have a lot of dots, and who has none?

The faculty of Harriet Tubman Academy for Social Justice did this activity and noted that just under 10% of their student population had no dots at all. They also noted that several students had eight or more dots. As one of the teachers said, "It's not just that the 'lots of dots' students are popular or easy to like. Some of them were our focus last year or the year before. And it's worked because look how connected they are now. And some, like Karla, really need all of those connections. I can't imagine her life without each of the people represented by those dots advocating for her."

22% of students tell us they have difficulty fitting in at school.

The teachers at Tubman also spent time during their professional learning session talking about what they knew about the students who received no dots. Many of them were absent a lot. All of them lived in poverty. Most of them were generally well-behaved and "flew under the radar," as one of the teachers commented. They decided that the first period teachers for each of these students would learn more about them and that the staff would meet as a group in three weeks to share their findings. The first period teacher was tasked with identifying the student's interests, aspirations, history, and current academic status across classes.

Three weeks later, each of the students with no dots was profiled by a first period teacher. Based on what they learned, they identified specific adults who could start to develop a relationship. They made matches based on interests and personality. In some cases, the first period teacher suggested that they skip a student because, as one of them said, "We don't need to worry any more about Thomas. It's just been three weeks, but we're already connected and he's coming early to school to talk with me further. He has my dot now and I think he'll have yours soon enough." They committed to devote additional professional learning time to reviewing student progress and monitoring students who, at the middle of the year, were not connected to any adults in the school.

There are a number of additional tools teachers can use to develop this aspect of their relationship with students. Some people recommend an interest survey. These are easily created by teachers to find out what their students like to do in their free time, which topics they find interesting, and what their hobbies are. Others recommend sharing parts of your life with students. We see value in both of these activities and a range of other things that teachers do to ensure that they, and their classrooms, are inviting.

Having an uninviting teacher or classroom can shut down a lot of learning. And, sadly, we've all been there. But being invitational only goes so far. It is a necessary component, but it is insufficient to ensure that teacher-student relationships result in increased learning.

The Equitable Aspect of Teacher-Student Relationships

The second component of strong teacher-student relationships requires a focus on equity. Students notice differential treatment, and they know who the teacher likes and does not like. That's not to say that teachers should not differentiate curriculum and instruction; they should. But the relationships between teachers and students is not one of the areas to consider for differentiation. Every student in the class needs a fair chance to develop a healthy relationship with the teacher. Of course, some students are more likeable than others, and some are really good at proactively developing a relationship with you. But others don't yet have the tools in their toolkit. It's up to you to initiate and cultivate productive relationships, even with the hardest to reach kids. We're not selecting our friends; we're teaching youngsters. Accordingly, we work hard to develop equitable relationships with all of our students. One of the ways to do that is to monitor behavior patterns that unintentionally send students messages that they are not valued or not liked. Those behavior patterns are beautifully articulated through a program that has endured for three decades.

More than 30 years ago, staff from Los Angeles County Office of Education decided to address the issue of inequities. They reviewed the available research and identified 15 factors, or interactions, that can facilitate student achievement. These interactions connect to student achievement and are known as **Teacher Expectations and Student Achievement** or TESA. The research for their model has been updated regularly, but the 15 interactions have remained constant. The 15 interactions can be found in Figure 2.2. A summary of each interaction can be found in Figure 2.3.

Although the TESA model focuses on students who are not performing at grade level for any reason, our work focuses on using the TESA interactions to develop positive and equitable teacher-student relationships with all students. Below, we'll discuss each of the 15 interactions and

TEACHER EXPECTATIONS AND STUDENT ACHIEVEMENT (TESA) INTERACTION MODEL

TESA
Teacher Expectations & Student Achievement

TESA Interaction Model

UNITS	A Response Opportunities	B Feedback	C Personal Regard
	Strand		
1	Equitable Distribution	Affirm/Correct	Proximity
2	Individual Help	Praise	Courtesy
3	Latency	Reasons for Praise	Personal Interest and Compliments
4	Delving	Listening	Touching
5	Higher-Level Questioning	Accepting Feelings	Desist

Source: Los Angeles County Office of Education,
http://www.lacoe.edu/SchoolImprovement/StateFederalPrograms/SFPPublications.aspx

Figure 2.2

why they are important. As you can see, TESA consists of three main strands:

- response opportunities
- feedback
- personal regard

Each of the strands goes deeper as you progress down the units. Our goal in presenting this information is for you to think about your classroom and how your behaviors, actions, and interactions can facilitate students' learning. Each of these interactions requires that teachers

FIFTEEN INTERACTIONS FOR TEACHER EXPECTATIONS AND STUDENT ACHIEVEMENT (TESA)

Equitable Distribution of Response Opportunity. The teacher learns how to provide an opportunity for all students to respond or perform in classroom learning situations.

Affirmation or Correction. The teacher learns how to give feedback to students about their classroom performance.

Proximity. The teacher learns the significance of being physically close to students as they work.

Individual Helping. The teacher learns how to provide individual help to each student.

Praise for the Learning Performance. The teacher learns how to praise the students' learning performance.

Courtesy. The teacher learns how to use expressions of courtesy in interactions with students.

Latency. The teacher learns how to allow the student enough time to think over a question before assisting the student or ending the opportunity to respond.

Reasons for Praise. The teacher learns how to give useful feedback for the students' learning performance.

Personal Interest Statements and Compliments. The teacher learns how to ask questions, give compliments, or make statements related to a student's personal interest or experiences.

Delving, Rephrasing, Giving Clues. The teacher learns how to provide additional information to help the student respond to a question.

Listening. The teacher learns how to apply active listening techniques with students.

Touching. The teacher learns how to touch students in a respectful, appropriate, and friendly manner.

Higher-Level Questioning. The teacher learns how to ask challenging questions that require students to do more than simply recall information.

Accepting Feelings. The teacher learns how to recognize and accept students' feelings in a nonevaluative manner.

Desisting. The teacher learns how to stop a student's misbehavior in a calm and courteous manner.

Source: Los Angeles County Office of Education.

Figure 2.3

develop strong relationships with students. But we present these not simply to list them but to equip you with a means of analyzing a relationship that needs strengthening. We challenge you to choose one student who is among the hardest to reach and another with whom you have a strong and positive relationship. Now collect data for a few days about each time you interact with them. Is it possible that you have far fewer interactions with the hard-to-reach student? TESA data bear witness to this phenomenon. Without intending to, we often have noticeably fewer interactions with those students who are academically or behaviorally problematic. And it's difficult to build a relationship with a relative stranger.

1. Equitable Distribution of Response Opportunity

The first interaction focuses on the students who are encouraged to participate in class. Research evidence suggests teachers call on lower-performing students less often than higher-achieving ones. Teachers also call on more boys than girls and on students with whom they have stronger relationships. Some students sit quietly in class and are never asked to participate by the teachers. Some teachers report that this is so that students won't be embarrassed. Other say it is because students may not understand the content or the language and thus can't answer the questions or participate in the discussion. However, students interpret a lack of response opportunity as evidence that the teacher doesn't believe in them or doesn't like them. This factor requires that teachers analyze the patterns of students who are asked to participate in the class and then identify students who routinely are not invited to participate so that they can change it.

2. Affirmation or Correction

When students do participate in the class, they want to know what their teachers think about their responses. At minimum, teachers should acknowledge the response—whether it is orally, in writing, on a test, or on a project. We know that students gauge their teachers' reactions to their participation and make decisions about future participation based on this information. If incorrect information is presented, students expect that teachers will correct them, but in ways that honor them as individuals. Unfortunately, lower-achieving students are often ignored or do not receive feedback. All students deserve affirmation and corrections, yet only 62% of students report

Only 62% of students report that teachers help them learn from their mistakes.

that teachers help them learn from their mistakes. These corrections must be responsive to the students' current language development and skill level, while clearly communicating increased performance expectations. Importantly, we know that constant correction can lead to low self-esteem and poor performance. The effective teacher balances affirmation and correction to facilitate student learning.

3. Proximity

The physical presence of the teacher in the classroom is a powerful motivator. We know that teachers use proximity as a classroom management tool. Proximity also communicates value. Teachers often stand near students who perform well, students with whom they have a strong relationship, or temporarily when students are in trouble behaviorally. In terms of seating patterns, lower-achieving students are typically placed (or are allowed to sit) in the back of the room or in the corners. On the other hand, students who have stronger relationships with the teacher are often found in the front and down the center of the room. The goal of this interaction is to ensure that the teacher gets physically near each of his or her students. This communicates value and provides the teacher an opportunity to develop a bond with each individual.

4. Individual Helping

Most teachers know that students who are struggling in school need individual help to succeed. However, students who are performing at grade level and students above grade level typically are far more assertive in seeking the teacher's assistance. In addition, teachers tend to provide more individual help for students they like better or with whom they have strong relationships. This TESA factor reminds us to focus our instructional intentions and interventions equitably. Consistent with Vygotsky's (1978) theory of the Zone of Proximal Development, every student needs access to an adult model who can facilitate learning.

> 26% of students share they have never been recognized for something positive at school.

5. Praise for the Learning Performance

Everyone likes to hear praise. As humans, we like to know when we do something well. For students who find school difficult, praise is especially important. Unfortunately, in too many class-rooms, praise is reserved for students who have a positive relationship with the teacher, and 26% of students share they have *never* been recognized for something positive at school. Importantly, the verbal praise must match the nonverbal cues that the student is receiving. These nonverbal cues include looking at the student, tone of voice, using the student's name, facial expressions, and authenticity. It is also important to note that praise builds the bond between the teacher and his or her students. Figure 2.4 includes a number of ways for teachers to say "good job."

> Only 58% of students believe teachers respect students.

6. Courtesy

Although it may seem obvious that we should interact with students in a courteous way, research indicates that teachers do not always do so, especially when students come from traditionally underrepresented ethnic groups. There is evidence that English learners, for example, are treated and spoken to harshly. For example, Cesar Chavez reported having to wear a sign in school that said, "I am stupid. I speak Spanish." Although this incident took place many years ago, it is not so very different from an attitude still prevalent today. As teachers, we must remember that our interactions with students leave lasting impressions in their mind about who they are and what they can do. At the very minimum, every student deserves respect and courtesy, but only 58% of students believe teachers respect students. Ideally, every student knows that he or she is loved and valued.

7. Latency

Wait time, or latency, refers to the amount of time between the teacher asking a question and then either moving on or answering the question himself or herself. There are a number of benefits to ensuring that students are provided at least a five-second wait time before the teacher moves on, calls on someone else, or answers the question himself or herself. Providing students with sufficient time ensures that the variety of students who volunteer to answer will increase, as will the length of their responses. In addition, there is evidence that providing appropriate wait time results in responses that demonstrate critical thinking and are supported by evidence or logic. Wait time can be

Video 5
The Importance
of Wait Time

resources.corwin.com/
engagementbydesign

WAYS TO SAY "GOOD JOB"

Aren't you proud of yourself?	Much better!	Well, look at you go.
Bravo!	Nice going.	Wonderful!
Congratulations!	Nothing can stop you now.	Wow!
Congratulations. You got it right!	Now that's what I call a fine job.	You are learning fast.
Couldn't have done it better myself.	Now you have it!	You are really learning a lot.
Exactly right.	Now you have the hang of it.	You are very good at that.
Excellent!	Now you've figured it out.	You certainly did well today.
Fantastic!	One more time and you'll have it.	You did a lot of work today.
Fine!	Outstanding!	You did it that time!
Good for you!	Perfect!	You did that very well.
Good going.	Right on!	You figured that out fast.
Good job, [person's name].	Sensational!	You have great potential.
Good remembering.	Super!	You haven't missed a thing!
Good thinking.	Superb!	You must have been practicing.
How impressive!	Terrific!	You outdid yourself today!
I knew you could do it.	That kind of work makes me happy.	You really make my job fun.
I like that.	That was first-class work.	You remembered!
I think you're doing the right thing.	That's better than ever.	You're doing a good job.
I think you've got it now.	That's coming along nicely.	You're doing beautifully!
I'm happy to see you working.	That's how to handle that.	You're doing fine!
I'm proud of the way you worked today.	That's it!	You're doing that much better today.
I'm very proud of you.	That's much, much better!	You're getting better every day.
I've never seen anyone do it better.	That's quite an improvement.	You're improving.
It's such a pleasure to teach when you . . .	That's right!	You're on the right track now!
Keep it up!	That's the best ever.	You're really going to town.
Keep on trying.	That's the best you've ever done.	You're really improving.
Keep up the good work.	That's the right way to do it.	You're really working hard today.
Keep working on it.	That's the way!	You've got it made.
Kudos!	That's the way to do it.	You've got that down pat.
Marvelous!	Tremendous!	You've just about got it.
	Way to go!	You've just about mastered it.

Figure 2.4

useful for curbing the propensity of some students who quickly arrive at an answer and are always sharing. This isn't the student's fault, by the way. It occurs when we're not closely monitoring distribution of response opportunities (see TESA #1). Posing questions differently, such as saying, *"I have a question for you, and I want you to think about it and give me a thumbs up when you believe you have an answer,"* signals to students that you are interested in their collective thinking, not just the one who got it the quickest. In addition to the latency period between asking a question and expecting a response, teachers should wait for the student to finish and let the response linger in the air for one or two seconds. This gives everyone in the room an opportunity to consider what was just said. We're sure you have been part of a conversation in which the person you're talking to has clearly already formulated his or her response. What happens to you? It makes you want to curtail your conversation in frustration. And we don't want that for students.

8. Reasons for Praise

As we delve deeper into the TESA interactions, we note that students also need reasons for the praise they receive. When possible, praise should be based on a specific action or response. The recommendation from TESA is that we strive for a ratio of four praises for each correction. Barely half (53%) of students say their teachers recognize them when they try their best . . . and we are *certain* we can do better than that! We can shape or influence students' thinking when we provide specific reasons for the praise they receive. TESA recommends that praise should

Video 6
The Importance of Praise

*resources.corwin.com/
engagementbydesign*

- Immediately follow the accomplishment

- Be specific to the accomplishment

- Be informative or appreciative

- Be varied and credible

- Be natural rather than theatrical

- Be individualized

- Be attributed to effort and ability (Los Angeles County Office of Education, 2002, p. D-31)

Video 7
Integrating Students'
Personal Interests

*resources.corwin.com/
engagementbydesign*

9. Personal Interest Statements and Compliments

Another way we make connections with our students and show them that we care is by making statements that indicate that we have a personal interest in their life. It may be as simple as noting that *"Arian, you're from the same state where this story takes place. I'd like to hear from you later about whether the author's description jibes with your own impressions."* Teachers may also ask students to share their experiences and backgrounds when they are connected to the focus of the class. In addition, teachers can pay compliments to students about performance at a sports event, their effort, or anything else the student engages in. In doing so, the student knows that the teacher has taken personal interest and cares enough to remember. These personal statements and compliments establish and maintain healthy relationships between teachers and students. We are hopeful that employing strategies such as these will help us to increase the percentage of students who believe teachers care about them as an individual (currently 53%).

10. Delving, Rephrasing, Giving Clues

As we have already noted, teachers tend to ask fewer questions of low-achieving students than higher-achieving students. They also interact less frequently with students with whom they have limited or weak relationships. In addition, when teachers ask low-achieving students a question, they typically pose easier questions or excuse them from answering if they hesitate, look confused, or avert their eyes. As if this were not enough, teachers tend to rephrase the question less often for lower-achieving students and rarely give students who are less valued clues to be able to answer. When students are asked "easy" questions, it reinforces for the teacher that the student doesn't know much. It also sends a message to the student that the teacher doesn't expect much. We are not suggesting that teachers only ask difficult questions; rather, we hope that teachers scaffold their questions and provide the supports necessary for students to successfully respond in the classroom. We know that leveling questions is a good practice, provided that teachers give students opportunities to stretch their thinking, rephrase questions as necessary to aid students' understanding, and give students clues rather than pass over them to another student.

11. Listening

We know that listening is a critical skill. Unfortunately, students spend a great deal of their class time listening and not engaging in other literacy skills and practices. Several decades ago, Flanders (1970) noted that teachers of high-achieving students talked about 55% of the class time. He compared that with teachers of low-achieving students who monopolized class, talking at least 80% of the time. Clearly, as teachers, we need to listen more. As listeners, we give our attention to the person speaking, make eye contact with that person, engage in nonverbal clues that we understand, and can ask questions or make comments about what the person said. These listening skills build and maintain relationships between people, and students want to be listened to by their teachers. Currently, 43% of students report that adults in their school listen to students. When students *are* listened to, it facilitates the bond between teacher and student and lets them know that they are valued.

12. Touching

We are respectful of cultural and gendered customs around touching, and we must first state that consideration for students and teachers is essential. Having said that, TESA challenges assumptions about physical contact and suggests that many students respond to respectful touch. The relationships that develop when teachers can shake the hand of a student entering the room, place a hand on a student's shoulder to communicate that he or she is doing a great job, or "high-five" a student who has completed a major project are amazing. In addition, it should be noted that teachers can "touch" with their eyes and words—the wink of an eye for a job well done, a smile at the end of the presentation, the use of pronouns such as *we* and *our* all communicate value and respect. But if you are not comfortable with physical contact, be

Clearly, as teachers, we need to listen more.

43% of students report that adults in their school listen to students.

consistent. In other words, if you shake hands with some students, offer it to all students. As we have noted before, students are watching and they notice when inequitable relationships develop. Students who are not greeted with a high-five notice those who are and believe that they are less important.

TESA challenges assumptions about physical contact and suggests that many students respond to respectful touch.

13. Higher-Level Questioning

As we have noted before in this discussion of the TESA interactions, teachers generally ask fewer and easier questions of students who struggle at school. Importantly, this does not foster their critical and creative thinking. Students should also have opportunities to develop skills in asking questions to seek clarity or further explore things they are curious about. Fifty-eight percent of students say they feel comfortable asking questions in class. That means that 42%—a significant portion of a classroom—do not. They are in need of strategies and support from teachers to use their voice in both answering questions and asking them.

Every student needs the opportunity to engage in complex thinking and receive the support to do so. To ensure that students develop cognitive flexibility, teachers need to create good questions on the spot that expand student thinking.

14. Accepting Feelings

We react to the world around us. As teachers, we need to accept the feelings of our students. As stated in Chapter 1, 43% of students believe that teachers care about their problems and feelings. We must acknowledge their joys and sorrows. And we can help them think about their emotions and how to channel them. Teachers can create an environment that is safe for learning, which requires that we attend to students' emotional lives. Over the course of the year, students experience a wide range of emotions such as grief over the loss of loved ones, the excitement of a new living arrangement, embarrassment over mistakes, and joy when acknowledged for work well done. As teachers, we must be on the lookout for these feelings, help our students name them, and assist students in deciding what they want to do with these feelings.

As human beings develop stronger relationships, feelings and moods are easier to detect.

15. Desisting

The final interaction outlined by TESA focuses on the actions that teachers take to stop misbehavior. Most teachers use a wide range of strategies to manage their classrooms. In too many classrooms, lower-achieving students are punished more frequently. Desisting should be impartial and equitable. The teacher must clearly demonstrate that he or she expects the same behavior and interest in learning from all students. Regardless of the systems in place, an effective teacher knows that the desired outcomes of desisting are to end the problem behavior while maintaining continued respect for the learner.

58% of students say they feel comfortable asking questions in class.

Addressing each of these 15 interaction factors that comprise the TESA model contributes to a positive classroom environment and fosters healthy, productive relationships between students and teachers. From this discussion of interactions, we hope that it is clear that teachers must hold high expectations for all students and they must strive to develop constructive relationships with students. Unfortunately, teachers don't always have, or communicate, the same expectations for all of their students.

How Teachers Communicate Expectations Differentially

For all of our good intentions, we are vulnerable to subconsciously telegraphing messages to students that we don't hold them all in the same regard or have consistently high expectations for them as individuals. The opening days of school are inspiring. At the outset of the year, teachers strive to establish positive relationships with students. But after the first blush of early fall gives way to winter, these efforts tend to fall to the wayside. Instead, these initially positive efforts stand in stark contrast to what occurs all too often, and as the year unfolds, teachers begin to project differential levels of expectations on students. Consider the findings of Good (1987), based on two decades of research on teacher behaviors (see Figure 2.5 for a complete list). As teachers begin to sort out who are the "high achievers" and the "low achievers," they exhibit markedly different ways of interacting with their students. Compared to those identified as "high achievers," those who are "low achievers" get less wait time to answer questions, are criticized more often, are seated farther away from the teacher (thus creating a physical distancing), and are given less eye contact by the teacher.

Lower expectations are manifested in subtle ways. Although the teachers themselves may believe that their expectations are consistently high for all their students, the evidence is that they are not. The hard truth is that differential expectations of students correlate to race, ethnicity, language ability, and socioeconomic status (McKown & Weinstein, 2008; Parker, Jerrim, Schoon, & Marsh, 2016). The teacher's intentions may be admirable. He or she doesn't want to embarrass students by asking them questions that require them to express a complete thought, or frustrate them by giving them a difficult assignment, or inhibit them by correcting errors using feedback. The seemingly minor interchange between teacher and student can either hold students to high expectations or allow them to sit in silence and become passive learners while the teacher turns to another student for the answer. In truth, we may be loving our low-achieving students to death, in a misguided effort to remove any hint of challenge. The following two exchanges illustrate how questioning approaches can elicit different responses, as a small group of young children look at pictures to generate oral language:

T: *Jackson, what is going on in this picture?*

S: *[no response]*

T: *What are the children doing [in the picture]?*

S: *Boy.*

T: *Esther, can you tell us what the children are doing?*

After asking the question and rewording it once, the teacher moves on to another student, perhaps feeling uncomfortable about putting the child on the spot when he is unable to come up with an answer, or

> Teachers can create an environment that is safe for learning, which requires that we attend to students' emotional lives.

BEHAVIORS THAT CAN INDICATE DIFFERENTIAL TEACHER TREATMENTS OF HIGH AND LOW ACHIEVERS

- Waiting less time for low achievers to answer
- Giving low achievers answers or calling on someone else rather than trying to improve their responses by giving clues or rephrasing questions
- Rewarding inappropriate behavior or incorrect answers by low achievers
- Criticizing low achievers more than high achievers for failure
- Praising low achievers less frequently than high achievers for success
- Failing to give feedback to the public responses of low achievers
- Paying less attention to low achievers or interacting with them less frequently
- Calling on low achievers less often to respond to questions
- Seating low achievers farther away from the teacher
- Demanding less from low achievers
- Interacting with low achievers more privately than publicly and monitoring and structuring their activities more closely
- Giving high achievers more than low achievers the benefit of the doubt when grading tests or assignments
- Having fewer friendly interactions with low achievers
- Providing briefer and less informative feedback to the questions of low achievers
- Making less eye contact and other forms of nonverbal communication with low achievers
- Providing less time on instructional methods with low achievers when time is limited
- Not accepting or using low achievers' ideas

Source: Adapted from Good, T. L. (1987). Two decades of research on teacher expectations: Findings and future directions. *Journal of Teacher Education, 38*(4), 32–47.

Figure 2.5

perhaps feeling pressured for time and wanting to maintain the pace of the lesson. But look at what a difference persistence can make:

T: *Madison, what do you think the children in this picture are feeling?*

S: *[No response]*

T: *Look at their faces. What do you think they are feeling?*

S: *Sad.*

T: *Why would they be sad?*

S: *[No response]*

T: *What is the clue in the picture that tells you why they might be sad?*

S: *The ball is over the fence.*

T: *Why would that make them sad?*

S: *They can't reach the ball.*

T: *Put those ideas together.*

S: *The children are sad 'cause the ball is over the fence. They can't play with it.*

The second exchange took a minute longer than the first. In terms of technique, the teacher used prompts and cues to scaffold Madison's answer. But what's also interesting is that both exchanges occurred within minutes of one another during a small group lesson with kindergartners. Without intending to, the teacher telegraphed the message that she expected far less of Jackson than she did of Madison.

The Advocacy Aspect of Teacher-Student Relationships

In addition to being inviting and equitable, teachers with strong relationships with their students are *advocates*. They believe in their students and want what's best for them. Although every teacher we have talked with agrees, only 73% of students think their teachers believe in them. The other 27% of students desperately need to know they are cared for and that we believe in them. We are reminded of a quote from the eminent child psychologist Urie Bronfenbrenner: "Every child needs an adult who is crazy about him (or her) in order to grow up" (cited in Penn, 2008, p. 46). We think Bronfenbrenner selected his words wisely. He did not say that some children needed this; he said *every* child. To grow up, children need advocates who will go to great lengths to ensure that they are successful. Bronfenbrenner

> Only 73% of students think their teachers believe in them.

also said *crazy*, which is interesting. We take this to mean that the adult loves the child unconditionally and puts aside some rational/logical thinking in pursuit of what is right for the child. We're not suggesting that teachers break the law, but Bronfenbrenner reminds us that we should go pretty far to protect the students that society has charged us with educating. Importantly, it's not just physical protection that our students need. Physical protection is important, but so is psychological, social, and emotional well-being. As advocates for children and youth, we strive to protect them from harm while they are in our care. Yes, we are temporary members of their lives, and their families have an important role to play in helping children grow up. But while they are with us, they must be safe—safe to experiment, express themselves, and grow.

Sometimes the teacher-student relationship requires advocacy with other adults. For example, Tammy was scolded for not returning the playground equipment, but she wasn't given a chance to explain. Later that day, she told her second-grade teacher that another student had just taken the ball and cones and thrown them on the field, after Tammy had just picked them up. Tammy's teacher asked the playground supervisor to come to the classroom so that Tammy could explain what happened. This well-meaning adult apologized to Tammy and promised to ask if there were other events preventing students from following rules in any future situations. The playground supervisor also thanked Tammy's teacher for her advocacy, saying, *"We only get better when we understand situations. I learned from this, so I thank you."*

Other times, teachers have to advocate for their students through legal channels. When students trust their teachers, they tell them when they are hurt. The injury may be physical or emotional. And it's the teacher's responsibility to advocate for the student and work to make things right. Unfortunately, this means that students sometimes tell their teachers about abuse they have suffered. In these cases, the teacher has to advocate for the student by informing the proper authorities. It's painful but important. The relationship is maintained when the student knows that there are adults who care enough to take action. We could tell any number of stories of students sharing terrible situations with us, but

> "Every child needs an adult who is crazy about him (or her) in order to grow up."
>
> —Urie Bronfenbrenner

suffice it to say that there are lots of young people who have experienced horrors, and when they turn to you for help, you must act even as it breaks your heart.

Bullying and cyberbullying are issues that demand teacher advocacy for students. The national Student Voice data show that 40% of students report that bullying is a problem at their school. Some groups are at heightened risk, especially those who are perceived to be lesbian, gay, bisexual, transgender, queer, or gender nonconforming (LGBTQ+; Schneider, O'Donnell, Stueve, & Coulter, 2012). Teachers do not need to wait for students to tell them that they have been bullied. We suggest that teachers engage students in developmentally appropriate lessons about bullying and cyberbullying and make it clear that it will not be tolerated. These open conversations signal to students that you are open and receptive to their concerns. (A good resource for instructional materials about bullying is http://www.pacer.org/bullying/resources/toolkits.) In addition, schools can sign up for an anonymous reporting system, such as Sprigeo (http://www.sprigeo.com), so that students can report situations to people who can address the issues.

Restorative Practices

Even when bullying is not the issue, relationships are damaged. Invariably, humans cause harm to one another. Sometimes they mean to, and sometimes it is unintentional. Regardless, harm has been done. Teachers compromise their relationships with students when they fail to acknowledge and address the harm that their students experience. It's dismissive to say, *"Shake it off like a man"* (a comment loaded with gendered stereotypes) or *"Let it go; it wasn't that bad."* Over time, when harm is not addressed, students come to believe that their teachers do not care about them, and they start to withdraw from the learning environment. We also know from personal experience that addressing harm can consume a lot of classroom time, and we recognize that there has to be a balance. Restorative practices are a promising practice in building relationships and addressing harm (Anyon et al., 2016). One of the more effective ways that we have seen teachers address harm is through the use of circles, in which students are empowered to share their thinking.

Circles

Circle processes are part of the larger restorative practices model for helping students deal with harm. There are a number of types of circles, from those that require each student to speak, to those that allow for volunteers around the circle to speak, and those that designate a smaller group to sit inside a "fishbowl" to share their thinking. What they have in common is that students understand that there is a time in the day or week when they can share their experiences. At the start of the year, we recommend that the topics of discussion focus on routines, procedures, and class content. Students need time to acclimate to the process and to develop trust with the people in the room.

The students in Wendy Saul's third-grade class meet in a circle every day after lunch. As she notes, "I'm not worried about instructional minutes being spent on this for a few reasons. First, they're practicing language. Second, if they are really upset by something, they probably aren't learning the content. And third, the circles don't really take that long, and I can address most of the behavioral issues during the circle, which makes the rest of my day smoother."

During a circle in the first part of the year, Ms. Saul asked students to share their goals for the upcoming month. Brandi said that she wanted to improve her writing. Michael said that he wanted to get faster at multiplication. Anna said that she wanted to jump rope 100 times without touching the rope. Each student had a goal and heard the goals of his or her classmates. As the circle ended, Ms. Saul invited her students to return to their desks and write a plan to meet the goal that they had set for themselves.

Later in the year, Ms. Saul provided her students with opportunities to talk about "ways to improve our learning experience." When it was Henry's turn, he talked about not being allowed to play kickball and how that made him feel. Ms. Saul took note of this to talk with him further. But five students later, Armando said, *"I think it would be better if we let Henry play with us at recess. We didn't think he liked us, anyway. But he says some mean things, so we didn't let him play. But that's not being a good sport. Henry, you can play if you want. But can you stop saying mean things?"* Ms. Saul noted the exchange and made a point to talk with Henry about his language with others and to monitor the playground for a few days to see whether her students were more inclusive than they had apparently been.

Restorative Conversations

Sometimes, students harm each other, and they look to their teacher to help them repair the harm that has been done. The important thing about restorative practices is that students are provided an opportunity to learn how their actions impact others. They develop empathy as they come to realize that other people have feelings and that those feelings are damaged. Not all situations can be restored, we understand. But teachers, as advocates for their students, should know how to restore the relationships that their students damage. In doing so, the classroom becomes a more productive learning environment, and students begin to trust their teachers even more.

Restorative conversations are not about finding blame and punishing the offender; rather, they are an opportunity to make amends. That doesn't mean that offenders are not punished; they may be, depending on the severity of the harm they caused. In traditional discipline, it's the victim who is ignored. Once the adult believes that the investigation is complete, the victim rarely gets an opportunity to confront the perpetrator. The adult handles the punishment, which can further strain the relationship between the students.

A good restorative conversation provides the victim a chance to express how the event caused harm and what could be done to repair that harm. Victims are rarely ready to engage in this conversation right after they have been victimized and may need support from an adult in advance to be ready for the conversation. As part of the conversation, the perpetrator hears how victim was harmed and attempts to make amends for the situation, including a commitment to refrain from the action again. Restorative practices are not quick fixes to problematic behavior; rather, they are a long-term investment in students' relationships with others in the world. As such, well-implemented restorative practices require a whole school approach. Excellent resources and professional learning are available through the International Institute of Restorative Practices (www.iirp.org).

Loren and Haley never really seemed to get along. They each had a group of friends, and they talked about the other group constantly. Their put-downs escalated online, out of sight of their teachers. But one day, Loren was overheard making a very rude comment to Haley. Haley retorted with an equally ugly insult. Their teacher, Matt Turnbull, had a good relationship with both of these middle schoolers. He was shocked by their actions and asked to meet with them after school.

Sitting in the room, he shared what he had heard and how it made him feel. He asked each of the girls where their anger came from, but neither offered any clues. They agreed that they did not like each other, but they could not say why. The conversation did not seem to be going anywhere until Mr. Turnbull asked the girls whether they liked school. They both agreed that school was stressful because they worried about what the other would do if they were alone. As Loren said, *"Really, I could be doing better in school, but I spend a lot of time thinking about how to get back at Haley. And I worry about what she's saying about me behind my back. So really, school's not a great place for me."*

Mr. Turnbull decided to try the "If you knew me, you would know . . ." approach to see whether he could show the two girls that they were more alike than different. He asked each girl to complete the frame after he modeled, saying, *"If you knew me, you would know that I'm a dog lover. I have three of them and they take a lot of my time."*

The girls took turns, providing superficial responses such as *"If you knew me, you would know that my favorite color is yellow."* As they took turns, the information became more and more personal. At one point, Haley said, *"If you knew me, you would know that my dad is in jail."* Loren started crying, saying, *"That's something I'm afraid of. My dad doesn't live with us anymore because my mom says that he does illegal things. I really don't want him to go to jail."* They had found something in common.

Mr. Turnbull allowed them to continue talking for several minutes before interrupting. He said, *"Can you two make a commitment to me, and to each other, to squash this stuff? I know both of you as individuals, and it's just not who you are to me or to other people. You don't have to be friends, but could you make school a little better for each other? There really is no need to spend your day worrying about what the other person thinks or is saying, right?"* The girls agreed, with Haley adding, *"But I do think we're going to be friends now, and it will be so much better."*

Conclusion

Healthy, productive relationships make school a better place to be, for teachers, students, and leaders. It's hard to argue that teachers should not focus on developing strong relationships with their students, especially given the amount of time they are going to spend together over the year. In addition, there is good evidence that teacher-student relationships facilitate learning and are worth the time investment. If you ever doubt this, think about what happens when you run into students from years ago. What is the first thing that students say to you? "Do you remember me?" They always ask the same thing because they want to know whether the relationship mattered enough for them to be remembered. And when you tell them that you remember them, they talk about the things that you did to make them feel welcomed or invited into learning, how you were fair and equitable, and how you advocated for them while helping them grow.

Think about a teacher who made a significant impact on you. That teacher probably saw something in you that you didn't yet see in yourself, and she or he did so because you had a trusting relationship and that person was able to get to know you in a way that you didn't yet know yourself.

Yes, relationships matter.

CLARITY

Objectives
1. Discuss the influence
   of Islam in Southeast Asia
2. Describe th
   a form of
3. Explain the
   of oil to the
   and to th
4. Exp
   b

© Bob Daemmrich/PhotoEdit

This is the tale of two schools, both trying to ensure that their students learn. In both schools, teachers work hard. There are teachers on the campuses at six in the morning and teachers on the campuses at six in the evening. Students in both schools indicate that their teachers care for them and that they like being at school. Both schools serve a similar demographic of students, with about half of their students living in poverty and a wide range of languages spoken by the students. But these two schools realized very different results on every measure of student learning, from teacher-created progress monitoring tools to state assessments.

Walking through each school and talking with students about their learning revealed significant differences in the students' experiences in the classroom. In the first school—we'll call it Blossom Valley—the principal regularly stopped to talk with students, typically asking, *"What are you doing?"* Nearly every student queried related information about the task at hand. In the second school—we'll call it Mountain View— the principal asked students a different question: *"What are you learning?"* And nearly every student responded with a personal version of the learning expectation from the day.

This situation got us thinking about students' ownership of their learning. We believed that students at Blossom Valley were more focused on completing tasks whereas students at Mountain View were more focused on their learning. But given that the questions they asked were different, we asked the principals whether we could talk with students again. As we walked classrooms a second time, we asked students a consistent set of three questions:

1. What are you learning?
2. Why are you learning that?
3. How will you know that you have learned it?

The students at Blossom Valley had a very difficult time answering these questions. In most cases, they answered what they were doing rather than what they were learning. When asked why they were learning the content, the answers focused in three areas: (1) future events such as getting into college or getting a job; (2) the state standards; and (3) they had no idea. Not one of the Blossom Valley students could tell us how they would know if they learned the content. Some could describe how their teachers would know (e.g., looking at their homework, grading papers, giving a test).

This contrasted significantly with the student responses at Mountain View. Nearly every student we talked with could tell us what he or she was learning. They understood the daily learning intention but expressed it in their own words. For example, a group of students was studying life cycles. The learning intention on the board read "Students will recognize that insect life cycles are similar to and different from human life cycles." When asked what they were learning, Brandon said, *"I'm learning about life cycles, and today we're learning how butterflies are different from humans; like we don't lay eggs and butterflies do."* Rachael said, *"I'm learning about different life cycles. Humans are different from butterflies and frogs. Everything is born, but they're born in different ways. Like butterflies and frogs lay eggs, but people don't. And the butterfly life cycle has the chrysalis when they change a lot. Frogs change a lot from tadpoles that live only in the water. Humans don't change like that. We just grow bigger."*

When asked why they were learning the content, students' responses clustered into one of three categories:

1. **They would use this information outside of the classroom**. For example, Hasan said that he was learning about fractions *"so that I can measure things at home accurately,"* whereas Marla said that she was learning about fractions *"because people give you information that has fractions, like half past 10, and you need to know what it means."*

2. **They would learn about themselves**. For example, Michael said that part of the lesson on writing was so that he could *"learn about how I write and how my writing processes change because of the audience."* Tyler said that she was learning *"how I solve problems. The teacher has one way but it's not the only way. I have to learn about how I solve problems myself."*

> When students know what they are supposed to learn, why they are learning it, and how they will know that they have learned it, they learn more, behave better, and engage in school in more substantial ways.

3. **They needed to know this for future learning**. Tanya said, *"I'm learning these sight words so that I can read faster."* *"I'm learning sight words because they are in my books,"* Billy said. Andrew said, *"This is important to learn because if I don't understand the reasons that the colonists were not happy with Britain, then I might not understand the reasons for the American Revolution."*

And finally, when asked how they would know if they learned it, the vast majority of students at Mountain View described their personal use of the knowledge. Some talked about being able to teach others. Some talked about using their knowledge on projects and other assessments. Others said that they could tell their parents what they learned. And still others focused on feeling good about what they learned because they could remember the information.

It is probably no surprise that the students at Mountain View significantly outperformed the students at Blossom Valley academically. We attribute a significant part of this to the fact that their teachers were clear about the learning targets and made learning relevant. These teachers also had developed success criteria, and students had taken increased ownership of their learning. In other words, there was significant clarity in what students were learning. You might be surprised that the students at Mountain View also outperformed the students at Blossom Valley behaviorally. Mountain View students are subject to disciplinary action far less frequently than their counterparts at Blossom Valley. The suspension rates were also very different, with Mountain View experiencing fewer suspensions and no expulsions. Although this occurred at two elementary schools, it is equally applicable at middle and high school. It seems that when students know what they are supposed to learn, why they are learning it, and how they will know that they have learned it, they learn more, behave better, and engage in school in more substantial ways. The intersection between the teacher and the content—teacher clarity—contributes to student learning in valuable ways, and it further expands an engagement by design approach, which views the interaction between relationships, clarity, and challenge as imperative.

Clarity in Teaching

All of us are driven by purpose. When actions are attached to a purpose, we engage in a more meaningful way. We can compare our progress to the goal, make adjustments along the way, notice when we need help, and gauge our own success. Purpose transforms our actions from compliance to commitment, and it allows us to draw on intrinsic motivation to get the job done. Isn't that what we want for our students? Clarity in teaching is key to unlocking the curiosity and creativity that are essential traits for learning. But try as we might, the national Student Voice data tell a different story. Among high school students, only 57% responded positively to the statement, "School inspires me to learn," and only 38% agreed that "my classes help me understand what is happening in my everyday life." At a time when they are poised for adulthood, a significant number of young people are struggling to find the purpose of their school experiences.

Clarity in teaching is crucial if students are to accomplish the intended objectives in the classroom. To our thinking, teacher clarity consists of four essential elements:

- The teacher knows what students are supposed to be learning

- The teacher knows how students learn (pedagogical content knowledge)

- The students know what they are supposed to be learning

- The teacher and students know what success looks like

> Among high school students, only 57% responded positively to the statement, "School inspires me to learn." Only 38% agreed that "my classes help me understand what is happening in my everyday life."

Teacher clarity has a large effect size of 0.75 (Hattie, 2009), equivalent to nearly two years' worth of growth for a year in school. And that makes sense, doesn't it? When teacher and student are in agreement about what is to be learned and how both of them will know when intended learning has occurred, we save a whole lot of time that would have otherwise been spent floundering around looking for purpose.

A deep understanding of how students learn undergirds teacher clarity. Fendick (1990) describes four practices that ensure classroom instruction and assessment are properly marshaled, such that learners know what they are learning and how they can measure their own progress:

1. **Clarity of organization**: lesson tasks, assignments, and activities include links to the objectives and outcomes of learning

2. **Clarity of explanation**: information is relevant, accurate, and comprehensible to students

3. **Clarity of examples and guided practice**: the lesson includes information that is illustrative and illuminating as students gradually move to independence, making progress with less support from the teacher

4. **Clarity of assessment of student learning**: the teacher is regularly seeking out and acting upon the feedback he or she receives from students, especially through their verbal and written responses

This is the science of learning, and it marks the difference between a person with subject matter knowledge and one who possesses pedagogical content knowledge. Perhaps you have encountered this in your own education, when you enrolled in a course with a brilliant professor with deep knowledge of her subject but little understanding of how knowledge is developed in novices. A teacher needs subject matter knowledge, of course. It's difficult to conceive of an effective Algebra II teacher who doesn't understand the knowledge base. But at a 0.09 effect size (Hattie, 2009), the teachers' subject knowledge doesn't predict how well students will learn the content. The teacher also needs pedagogical knowledge, which is the science of teaching, and knowledge of how that interfaces with the subject being taught. That's pedagogical content knowledge (Shulman, 1987).

In this chapter, we will explain how to incorporate each of these four essential elements of teacher clarity into your teaching:

- Know *what* students are supposed to learn
- Know *how* students learn (pedagogical content knowledge)

> Purpose transforms our actions from compliance to commitment, and it allows us to draw on intrinsic motivation to get the job done. Isn't that what we want for our students?

- Know how to *communicate* what students will be learning

- Know how to develop *success criteria*

As we noted in Chapter 1, the *conceptual intersection* of the content and the teacher is an essential component of engagement by design.

Know What Students Are Supposed to Learn

It's impossible to plan a trip when you don't know your destination. Sure, you could wander through the landscape and encounter a few surprises along the way, but chances are that doesn't describe the kind of trip you usually take. The knowledge building we do with students has some parallels to a trip, in that we have some specific outcomes in mind, and we plan accordingly. These outcomes are articulated through the content standards, and although we promise this isn't a chapter about standards documents, it is important to acknowledge that they serve as a road map for teaching. Two assumptions are embedded in every standards document. The first is that the teacher holds an expectation that each child can meet and exceed the standards for the grade level or course. The second is that the teacher possesses an ability to organize the content such that skills and knowledge are built in a logical way. Seventy-three percent of students think their teachers believe in them and expect them to be successful. Our dream is that 100% of students will know without a single doubt that we believe in them and *know* they can be successful!

> **73% of students think their teachers believe in them and expect them to be successful.**

Communicate Expectations

When teachers communicate high expectations of students, they let learners know that they belong, that their teacher believes in their potential, and that the teacher's primary role is to help them achieve success. Teacher expectations have a powerful effect on learning. Hattie (2015) reports that teacher expectations of student learning have an effect size of 1.61, making it among the strongest overall of the nearly 200 effects examined and equivalent to three years' worth of growth for a year in school.

But how do teachers communicate expectations of students? In the previous chapter, we discussed monitoring the ways we interact with learners verbally and nonverbally such that we aren't differentially lowering expectations for some students (Good, 1987). One behavior of note in this context is the amount of public interaction we have with students who are not yet achieving at expected levels (we chose those words deliberately, as *yet* conveys optimism). When you engage a student in dialogue about the content, you are signaling to him and the rest of the class that he is valued as a learner. We don't mean interrogation, but rather true exploration of a learner's thoughts and perspectives that other students and the teacher can learn from. A low 47% of students believe teachers are willing to learn from them. A classroom is significantly transformed when students believe their participation in class is not just about getting a grade and they are truly engaged in a learning environment that values the thoughts of every individual as critical contributions to the collective learning of the class—including the teacher.

> **Only 47% of students believe teachers are willing to learn from them.**

We understand that some students are reluctant to share their ideas, especially if they have been socialized to believe that "doing school" is all about having the correct answer every time. So have a few tools in your arsenal:

- Give students time to consult with one another first in a small group before posing more complex questions

- Make sure you've got an equitable distribution of respondents

- Ensure that wait time is provided, both before and after the response

Lots of teachers pose a thought-provoking question, then ask their students to signal to them when they are ready to answer, such as giving a thumbs up. *"I see five people who are ready. Now it's seven. Keep thinking,"* says Kindergarten teacher Amy Washington. *"I'm seeing 12 people who are ready to answer,"* she continues. *"A few people aren't quite sure. Can you confer with your neighbor for a moment to check in?"* she asks. Next, Ms. Washington calls one of the children who took a bit longer to signal. "I want to be sure I'm not always calling on the same six kids who seem to have an answer right away," she said. "There's nothing wrong at all with giving ideas a chance to percolate."

Understand the Standards

One way to ensure that expectations for students are appropriate is to consult grade-level standards. These documents serve as a guide for the content students should master over the course of the year. Larry Ainsworth (2011) developed a process for helping teachers analyze standards to identify what students still need to learn. His recommended process begins with understanding the demands of a given standard or standards, which can be accomplished by listing the standard(s) and then identifying in each:

- *Verbs*—How students will demonstrate their understanding

- *Nouns*—What students are required to know

For example, second-grade students are expected to

Compare and contrast two or more versions of the same story (e.g., Cinderella stories) by different authors or from different cultures. (National Governors Association Center for Best Practices and Council of Chief State School Officers, 2010, p. 11)

The verbs tell us students need to compare and contrast. That means that students will have to understand the terms *compare* and *contrast.* They will also have to understand how to engage in compare and contrast activities cognitively. And they will have to use that knowledge in the context of reading. The nouns *versions, story, authors,* and *cultures* jump out. Again, students will need to understand the terminology and then how to use that information in analyzing a text. Hopefully, you can already see that this standard will require multiple lessons for students to eventually master. Many districts have engaged in extensive professional learning for teachers on analyzing standards. The true value of this work can be found in the deep understanding of groups who have engaged in such processes. More informally, there is much to be gained from working collaboratively with colleagues at your school in analyzing the standards to plan for learning.

As we plan instruction, we also consider the prerequisite knowledge, the key vocabulary (especially terms not included in the standard), as well as ideas for teaching and assessing. Figure 3.1 contains a planning tool that teachers can use to analyze standards for planning instruction. Returning to the second-grade standard above, the standard seems to assume that students know that there are different versions of the same stories. If they don't, instruction will likely need to start there. In addition, the standard requires that students know the difference between stories and informational texts. For this standard, students should already know the difference between characteristics of narrative versus expository texts. If they do not, then the unit of instruction will need to include that information as well. Moving along, in addition to the vocabulary within the standard, students might need to know the terms *point of view, characters, setting, problem, goal, message, moral, events, solution, plot, similarities, differences,* and so on. Instructional ideas could include teacher modeling using two versions of Cinderella as well as collaborative groups with various versions of Johnny Appleseed. Alternatively, the teacher might plan a series of lessons analyzing two texts using different perspectives each day, such as characters on the first day, setting on the next, goal the next, and so on. Assessment options include retellings, concept maps, written responses to writing prompts, and so on.

> # 67% of students believe what they are learning will benefit their future.

Our point here is that teacher clarity requires that teachers know what students are expected to learn. This requires maintaining high expectations for students and a deep understanding of the grade-level standards. Teachers should also be able to explain to students how these standards are helping prepare them for the future. Sixty-seven percent of students believe what they are learning will benefit their future. When students *do* understand the link between standards and the rest of their lives, the learning experience becomes all the more meaningful and engaging for students. Additionally, teacher clarity requires an assessment of students' current level of understanding.

Pre-Assess Understanding

As we have noted earlier, most standards have assumptions about students' prior learning. When that learning is absent, teachers have to

ANALYZING STANDARDS

Standard(s)	
Concepts (nouns)	**Skills (verbs)**
Prerequisite Knowledge	
Key Vocabulary	
Instructional Ideas	
Assessment Tools	

Figure 3.1

fill in the gaps. But there is another side to this coin. There are students who have already mastered specific aspects of the content, and it could be a waste of time for them to sit through another set of lessons. Thus, really knowing what students need to learn is more complex than simply analyzing standards. It also requires some sort of pre-assessment of students' knowledge. Of course, we don't want to squander too much time on this, but imagine the waste of time if students already understood the next unit of study.

Nancy and Doug had been teaching two large-section twelfth-grade English classes with more than 80 students in each class. One of the units required that students compare the opera *La Bohème* with the film and stage productions of the musical *Rent*. The reason we selected these texts related to the traveling Broadway production of *Rent*, which all students would be invited to attend. At the outset of the unit, we gave students a 10-item assessment focused on dramatic elements, consistent with the 12th-grade standards. For example, one question asked the following:

> The antagonist is the play's
>
> a. villain
>
> b. main character
>
> c. supporting character
>
> d. obstacle

Nearly every student answered this question correctly, which did not surprise us, as this content should have been covered before high school. Based on these data, there was really no reason for us to focus on this content. Had a large number of students incorrectly answered this question, we would have had to start the unit at a different place.

There are a number of ways to pre-assess students' understanding, and we are not advocating for total reliance on multiple choice items. We have used essays, constructed responses, retellings, visual representations, and performances to determine which aspects of the content students had already mastered. The point is not the specific tool, but rather an understanding of the gap between the grade-level expectations and

When students *do* understand the link between standards and the rest of their lives, the learning experience becomes all the more meaningful and engaging for students.

the current levels of performance for a group of students. When that gap has been identified, teachers can organize the content, and a series of lessons, in a logical sequence to ensure learning.

Organize Content

A skilled teacher understands the scope and sequence of the content being taught and knows how to convey skills and concepts in logical ways (Donovan & Bransford, 2005). The learning progressions featured in many standards documents organize content such that knowledge deepens over time, from surface learning to deep learning and then transfer (Fisher, Frey, & Hattie, 2016). The surface phase of learning describes time when students are learning the initial contours and boundaries of the topic, including fundamental principles and associated vocabulary. Students move into the deep learning phase when they begin to link concepts, see patterns, and build schema about the topic. The intent is to teach for transfer of knowledge; that is, the ability to apply learning to increasingly novel situations. These are not strictly developmentally based. In other words, it's not that primary students are in the surface phase, while middle schoolers are deepening knowledge, and lastly high school students are only about transfer. Rather, students cycle through these phases as they acquire new knowledge. Writing is a good example. Students should be continually learning new techniques to apply to their writing (surface), recognizing when writers are using similar techniques (deep), and utilizing them in their own writing (transfer). Primary writers may be moving through these phases as they learn about using descriptive language, and older students are similarly learning about argumentation and rhetoric. Expert teachers understand this progression and organize content learning such that students are able to acquire, consolidate, and apply knowledge.

Although surface, deep, and transfer phases unfold over weeks and months, attention to daily learning expectations is critical if students are to organize knowledge. Whether you call them learning intentions, learning targets, or purpose statements, the aim is the same: Describe what it is that students will be learning today. The daily purpose for learning is threefold:

- content purpose
- language purpose
- social purpose (Fisher & Frey, 2011)

Together, these describe the cognitive, linguistic, and behavioral objectives for the lesson. For instance, Margarita Espinoza's fifth-grade science lesson on stars includes the following purposes:

Content purpose: Understand that a star has a life cycle that begins with its formation and ends as a white dwarf.

Language purpose: Use star life cycle vocabulary (*stellar nebula, star, red giant, planetary nebula, white dwarf*) to describe the phases.

Social purpose: Collaborate with classmates to share information, ask questions, and listen closely.

Ms. Espinoza's purpose at this surface phase of learning in her science unit is to equip her students with fundamental principles and associated vocabulary. Later in the unit her purposes change, reflecting her students' progress into a deeper phase of learning. She is inviting them to link their current learning about stars and matter with knowledge previously learned about food webs:

Content purpose: Trace the path of matter in systems as it changes.

Language purpose: Compare and contrast how matter changes in the life cycle of a star and in a food web on Earth.

Social purpose: Ensure that each table partner has an opportunity to contribute to the discussion.

Later in the unit, they return again to conservation of matter, learned earlier in the year, to see how this principle applies in space as well as on Earth. This time, they are completing a lab experiment.

Content purpose: Investigate the relationship between a star's color and its density.

Language purpose: Develop a hypothesis and explain your reasoning in discussions and in writing.

Social purpose: Observe lab safety rules during your group's experiment.

As a result of her organization of the content and her attention to the daily purpose of each lesson, Ms. Espinoza's students are better able to understand the sequence of information about stars, further linking this to how energy and matter behave on Earth as well as in space. Her approach suggests that she is not simply marching through a prescribed curriculum with little thought to learning; she is able to "aim for surface and deep outcomes," an identified mind frame characteristic of expert teachers (Hattie, 2009, p. 5). In fact, in a large-scale comparative study of teachers who obtained National Board Certification (NBC) and those who applied but did not earn certification, the differential was their relative ability to move their students from surface to deeper learning (Smith, Baker, Hattie, & Bond, 2008). Although 74% of their students' work for NBC teachers was at the deep and transfer levels, only 29% of the student work submitted by noncompleters represented deep learning. In other words, experience only does not equate to expertise. Expert teachers have high expectations for their students and understand how to deepen knowledge.

> **74% of high school students report that their teachers "present lessons in different ways."**

Know How Students Learn

Earlier in the chapter, we introduced *pedagogical content knowledge*, which describes a teacher's ability to translate subject matter knowledge through pedagogy, that is, instruction. Teaching K–12 students effectively demands knowledge of child and adolescent development, as well as an understanding of how people learn. Although the concept of the blank slate has long been disproved, the lecture remains a primary approach to delivering content in some schools. But simply telling students is not the same as teaching them. People learn through a variety of channels, including demonstration and modeling, guided instruction, collaboration with peers, and opportunities to expand their learning independently, a system referred to as a "gradual release of responsibility" (Fisher & Frey, 2014). The good news is that the national Student Voice data suggest that the teaching methods used by teachers are varied, with 74% of high school students reporting that their teachers "present lessons in different ways."

Expert teachers inspire a level of psychological and emotional security among their students. They acknowledge that the learning at times will be difficult, but their students know they are in good hands. Hattie (2009) calls this "teacher credibility," and with an effect size of 0.90, it has an impressive impact on student learning. The four dimensions of teacher credibility are

- **Trust in the teacher.**

- **The perception that he or she is competent.** "One of the factors that increases trust is competence. We trust people who know what they are talking about and who deliver on what they promise. Students will be more inclined to trust teachers who provide the instruction and feedback they need to succeed" (Knight, 2016, p. 198).

- **Dynamism.** This is demonstrated by one's enthusiasm for the content. Sadly, only 38% of students report that teachers make school an exciting place to learn. And here's where relationships come in again.

- **Immediacy**. This is the ability to make connections with students using many of the interactions profiled in the last chapter in the section on Teacher Expectations and Student Achievement (TESA).

Your believability and authenticity are in play every moment of the day, and students are excellent barometers of credibility.

In this section, we will spotlight three concepts we consider to be crucial in thinking about the overlap between teachers and the content:

1. The ability to perceive content through the eyes of learners and respond accordingly through pedagogical content knowledge and **noticing**

2. An understanding of students' **prior knowledge** and the ability to leverage it for new learning

3. The belief that **errors** play an important role in learning and the teacher's stance toward seeking out and celebrating errors as opportunities to learn

Teacher Noticing

Teacher noticing is the ability to

- Notice the perspective of a student's thinking

- Interpret it as an indicator of what he or she knows

- Respond accordingly to advance his or her knowledge

But teacher noticing can be limited by what is known as the "expert blind spot." In a study that has been replicated several times, Nathan and Petrosino (2003) surveyed the understanding of early career secondary mathematics and science teachers about their students' foundational knowledge. These content experts had difficulty perceiving the cognitive trajectory their students needed to follow, relying instead on formal, abstract reasoning to introduce concepts. The researchers referred to this phenomenon as the "expert blind spot . . . that can lead people to assume that learning should follow the structure of the subject matter domain rather than the developmental needs and learning profiles of novices" (p. 909). In other words, a teacher's subject matter expertise is not sufficient. The fact is that these teachers, although well-versed in their disciplines, had forgotten what it was like to be a novice to the content. Expert teachers understand the learning perspectives of novice learners, notice their misconceptions, and are able to scaffold their understanding using concrete representations of concepts. It should be noted that the expert blind spot findings were similar among English language arts teachers (Grossman, 1990).

> Only 38% of students report that teachers make school an exciting place to learn.

The expert blind spot can leave students feeling—incorrectly—that they are not able to master the content. However, it is not because they can't grasp the material, but rather that the teacher's insufficient pedagogical content knowledge obscures his ability to see it through his student's eyes. On the other hand, teachers who are able to do so regularly employ the habit of noticing (Jacobs, Lamb, & Philipp, 2010). The ability to interpret students' cognition, including misconceptions and naïve understandings, and craft responses is a hallmark of an expert teacher. It's the assumption that what a child does, says, or writes makes sense, given what she currently knows. The teacher's purpose, then, is to rapidly hypothesize what gaps might exist and offer questions, prompts, or cues that move the student forward (Fisher & Frey, 2010). These interactions, which are primarily dialogic, form the core of formative assessment.

Kindergarten mathematics teacher Samantha Brownstein works with her student teacher, Jonas Lincoln, to develop his noticing skills. Ms. Brownstein presented the following problem to her students:

> Ava wants to make fresh orange juice for her family. She has 6 oranges. She needs 10 oranges. How many more does she need?

Ms. Brownstein was interested in seeing how her students might apply their mathematical thinking to solve this unfamiliar problem. When planning the lesson, she explained to her student teacher, "I'm curious to see whether they use the 10-frame we've been working with this year [a mat and counters with 10 boxes] and how they process the word *more.*"

Mr. Lincoln was puzzled by this. "Well, it's a subtraction problem, right? So they should be able to start with 10, take away 6, and come up with 4 as the answer."

Ms. Brownstein said, "Yes, you're right because you're thinking like a math expert. But they don't have those same formal logic skills. In their limited experience, 'more' means that you add. I anticipate that most of them will say 16 because they'll add the two numbers together. But there's some algebraic thinking that needs to happen. If that error happens, what would you deduce are the reasons?"

Mr. Lincoln thought for a moment. "So the problem is that they aren't seeing 'more' in the context of the problem. Using the 10-frame might help them visually represent the problem."

Ms. Brownstein replied, "There you go! That's what I want you to notice in this lesson. Not just *what* they are doing incorrectly but *why* they are doing it. It doesn't make sense to teach them the algorithm before they understand the concept. Based on what we see from our students, we'll go from there."

Prior Knowledge

Each student comes to the classroom with a host of experiences and knowledge, from both in school and out. Effective teachers actively seek an understanding of their students' prior knowledge, knowing that it is foundational to new learning. But it is more difficult to leverage students' prior knowledge if your relationships with them are not strong, if only because you have limited connections to them. In the last chapter, we discussed the importance of demonstrating interest in students' lives, which is an important source of information for gleaning past experiences. Their prior content knowledge is an equally important tool for developing student learning. Teachers can use a variety of tools, such as surveys and anticipation guides, to garner information about what students already know before a new unit of study is introduced.

Middle school English teacher Latrelle Peterson **surveys** her students regularly to find out information about their prior knowledge. "The students in my class are coming from seven different elementary schools, so I don't have a good handle on what they've done," explained Ms. Peterson. "So I start out the year with a survey on the learning management system for the class." Her first one, featured in Figure 3.2, asks students about their experiences with books that have been made into films. "It gives me something to immediately begin talking about with them, but it also lets them know that these stories came from somewhere. A lot of them are surprised that there's a book. That gives me a way to introduce them to some new reading," she said.

High school biology teacher Jorge Ramirez uses **anticipation guides** before a unit of study to learn about his students' prior knowledge. His anticipation guides usually feature between 5 and 10 statements about concepts related to the upcoming unit. Some of these statements are true, while others are false. "I don't get hung up on the technical details that I know they haven't learned yet, like the definition of an unfamiliar scientific term. But I do want to know about their understanding of major biological concepts," said Mr. Ramirez. Before teaching a unit on ecology, he posed statements that asked students to predict whether the population of a species would increase or decrease based on resource availability, population size, and density. "I get to see how it is that

ENGLISH CLASS SURVEY

	I have read this.	I have seen a movie version of this story.	I haven't read or seen it yet.
Hugo			
The Giver			
Hunger Games			
Stuart Little			
Charlotte's Web			
Little Women			
The BFG			
Charlie and the Chocolate Factory (Willy Wonka)			
I, Robot			
The Martian			
The Princess Bride			
The Jungle Book			
Harry Potter			
The Book Thief			
How to Train Your Dragon			
Diary of a Wimpy Kid			
The Chronicles of Narnia			

Figure 3.2

they're using what they already know to reason these scenarios," he said. "There's no grade, of course. They've come to expect that this is the way I kick off every unit."

Errors in Learning

Among the major achievements of the last decade is a growing appreciation for the role of errors in learning. The work of Dweck (2006), in particular, has assisted the field in understanding that errors are evidence of learning and that our responses to them contribute to a student's fixed or growth mindset. A student has a growth mindset when he or she understands that learning requires effort and that the learning process will include setbacks as he or she moves to mastery. A fixed mindset undermines his or her beliefs about learning, as the student attributes success to innate abilities, rather than effort. But it is important to say that these two constructs are on a continuum and are not an either/or proposition. All of us veer between these two mindsets, and they are situational. In other words, none of us is permanently in one corner or the other. Students aren't transformed into a growth mindset simply because we shift our praise from a focus on results to one on effort (although that is a good start).

Dweck (2006) cautions that all of us have triggers that send us back to a fixed mindset, such as trying something that is really outside our comfort zone. Therefore, being sensitive to what triggers a child, and then helping that student process it, is going to be more useful than just exhorting students to try harder. Our responses to their errors inform students about our belief in them. Thirty-three percent of students are afraid to try something new if they think they might fail. Supporting students in developing a growth mindset will help them embrace errors as an important part of the learning process.

High school mathematics teacher Kendra Gordon watches for such triggers with her students. "I get some kids who just freeze up when it comes to math," she said. "The mere mention of quadratic equations, and they've got this look of terror in their eyes," she said. Ms. Gordon began conferencing with her students a few years ago to help students move through these triggers. "Sometimes it's just a conversation about

> Errors are evidence of learning, and our responses to them contribute to a student's fixed or growth mindset.

something in their math past that we need to unpack," she said. "More often, we talk about what to do when you're stuck." Ms. Gordon makes sure that all her students have strategies for moving forward when they're stuck. "I model how I get stuck, and unstuck, as I confront problems and remind myself that some problems are going to take some time to resolve," she said. "I've also restructured my math classes so that we spend lots more time working collaboratively in small groups on rich mathematical tasks."

> **33% of students are afraid to try something new if they think they might fail.**

Ms. Gordon reinforces the role of errors as a necessary part of learning. "I remind them that we can either fail or fail forward. If we give up, all we've done is fail. End of story. But if we regroup and look at what went wrong and why, we can use it to figure out a new approach." The math teacher uses a technique called "My favorite mistake" several times a week. "I post problems that were solved incorrectly but had some great math concepts in use." Using an anonymous student's error, she and her class discuss what the mathematician did correctly and incorrectly and why that might have occurred. "It's shifting their perceptions about math, in that they can see that it's not just about whether the final answer was correct or not. It's appreciating all the sound mathematical thinking that did occur, too. Sometimes I use my own errors as examples." The teacher said that she is heartened by her students' responses. "There are times when a student will say, 'Hey, that's mine!' and it's said with confidence, not with shame."

Thus far, we have discussed two of the four major concepts related to clarity in this chapter: teachers know what students should learn, and they have knowledge of how students learn. In the next section, we turn our attention to the third, which is communicating to students what they are learning, why they are learning it, and how they can gauge their own progress.

Know How to Communicate What Students Will Be Learning

While reviewing research for the development of this book, we read a 2013 article in a peer-reviewed journal for college professors about ways to engage their students. We were struck by statements in the article that suggested it was essential to "keep students on their toes" by making their classes "unpredictable" to create "suspense and curiosity." We don't agree. Yes, classes should not be mundane and rote, such that every day feels like the same old slog. And there's nothing wrong with letting some activities be a surprise. But "unpredictable" seems to be about the worst descriptor of a classroom. It's in direct opposition to clarity. Students should always have a clear understanding of *what* they are learning and *how* they will be learning the content. Without this, we risk turning our students into passive, rather than active, learners.

Establishing Purpose

There are many purposes for learning that can be included in a lesson. Often, they are posted in classrooms so that students can refer to them throughout the lesson. As noted earlier in this chapter, purpose statements consist of three parts: the content purpose, the language purpose, and the social purpose. At a glance, students can preview the focus of the lesson even before class has started. However, posting is only the beginning. Each lesson includes time when the purpose statements are discussed, with conversation about tasks and activities associated with the purposes. Purpose statements are not agendas, which are schedules, although many teachers use both. But an agenda alone does not adequately communicate the learning intentions, instead leaving it up to the student to infer meaning. Purpose statements, on the other hand, communicate the learning intentions and serve a **cognitive priming function** as they alert the student to what will follow. Whenever possible, let students know how the concepts they are learning transfer to their life beyond school. Currently, 67% of students believe what they learn in school will benefit their future, a statistic we are certainly looking to increase. It should be noted that cognitive priming assists learners in transfer, a major goal of education (Wexler et al., 2016).

Video 8
Establishing Purpose

resources.corwin.com/ engagementbydesign

In addition to discussing the purpose statements at the start of the lesson, they should be reviewed when the class transitions between tasks. In the hurry to physically move to another area of the room, or cognitively to a different task, students are often more focused on the directions and logistics, rather than the learning. Before releasing students to their collaborative groups, fourth-grade teacher Deanna Lockwood returns to the purpose statements:

> *Remember what you're learning about today. We're learning about our state's history in this unit, and our content purpose today is to identify the ways humans altered the physical environment to meet their need for shelter, food, and security. Your language purpose is for your group to provide at least three examples in a paragraph of how native peoples and early settlers did this. That means your social purpose is to reach consensus about the three examples your group will be submitting. I want you to compare your results with the stated purpose and ask yourself whether you have achieved this. Because this is a 20-minute activity, I'll set the timer so you can pace yourselves. I'll be sitting in on each of your groups during this time.*

In doing so, Ms. Lockwood reinforces the learning intentions of the lesson and shifts their attention from compliance and task completion to metacognitive reflection. Later, after the children have reassembled as a class, the teacher returns to the purpose once again, this time as part of the closure. She reviews the statements, asking students to consider their own learning.

"We call them Minute Notes," she said. "I have them write their name on a sticky note and answer three questions. The first is for them to write about something new they learned in today's lesson. The second is a question they have about the content, language, or social purposes. The third is to write down anything they don't understand." Ms. Lockwood has a poster in the room with each child's name labeling a grid. "They post their sticky notes on the poster where their name is, and at a glance I can get a sense of what they know and still don't know. I usually review it when they're at recess and sort the notes into piles so I remember who I need to follow up with. I get quick info to plan tomorrow's lesson."

Giving Feedback

Communication about what is being learned doesn't begin and end with purpose statements. The ongoing feedback students receive serve as course correctors on their learning journey, guiding them back to the path when needed and altering the pace to match their progress. The effectiveness of feedback on student learning is large, at 0.75 (Hattie, 2009). Feedback about the cognitive and metacognitive processes students are using and the tasks they are completing will scaffold their learning. But feedback additionally signals to the student that he or she is worthy of the teacher's time and attention and the teacher believes in the student's learning potential. Your optimism and respect for students, as well as your high expectations for them, communicate your personal regard for them.

Students value the feedback they receive from teachers. In a 2016 poll administered by Gallup and the Northwest Evaluation Association, 74% of students in Grades 5 to 12 said that feedback in the moment was very helpful for their learning. But there is variance in the relative effectiveness of that feedback. *Timeliness* is essential, as feedback quickly grows stale. When it comes weeks after a written essay has been submitted, the feedback is nearly useless to the learner. The feedback should be *actionable*, meaning that the student is able to do something as a result. Feedback on a final assignment for a unit when further submissions are not possible is not useful. Far better to invest the time in providing feedback during development of the essay or project. Saving it for the end isn't feedback—it's evaluation. We used to make this same mistake, saving our very best feedback for the final product. Not only did it take seemingly forever to grade the assignments, but also the feedback we provided was neither actionable (as the assignment was done) nor useful (because there was little opportunity to apply it). We now use checklists to give rapid feedback during their drafts, and we save the grading (not feedback) for the final paper. In addition, the feedback should be *understandable* to the learner. When the feedback is developmentally or cognitively beyond the student's level of understanding, the feedback is not useful. (Think of those bewildering computer error messages you sometimes encounter. Here's our favorite: "Error Code 10: The

> 74% of students in Grades 5 to 12 said that feedback in the moment was very helpful for their learning.

environment is incorrect." What does *that* mean?) Finally, the feedback should reference the *goals* of learning. Therefore, linking the feedback to the purpose provides the student with a rationale for the feedback. Feedback that is timely, actionable, understandable, and goal-referenced gives the learner a path for improvement (Wiggins, 2012).

Feedback works on four different levels:

- **The task.** Provides the learner with information about the task, including whether it is correct, and gives directions such as, *"You will need to add a transition sentence at the end of this paragraph."*

- **The process.** Gives the student insight about the process being used. Adding the phrase *"so your reader will know what to expect next in your essay"* to the previous feedback example gives the student feedback about the task *and* the process she or he is using.

- **Self-regulation.** Focuses attention on the student's use of self-regulatory skills. *"As you re-read what you've written so far, compare it to the outline you made. Are you hitting your main points?"* reminds the learner about her or his ability to utilize strategies to achieve goals.

- **About the person.** Feedback about the person, often in the form of praise *("Nice job!"),* is the least effective of all. In contrast, feedback about process and self-regulation are the most effective kinds (Hattie & Timperley, 2007).

Much of the feedback offered to students comes in the form of in-the-moment conversations. But this can be a hit-or-miss proposition, as some students remain under your radar. Seventh-grade social studies teacher Tom Zhang tracked his own feedback habits over the course of a week and noticed that there were some students in each class period who rarely received any.

"That's when I decided to start conferencing with them," he said. Mr. Zhang explains that his class does quite a bit with document-based questions, especially for short constructed responses. "The kids work at their tables collaboratively to discuss the primary source documents. But what I've started doing is conferring with individual students

> Feedback signals to the student that he or she is worthy of the teacher's time and attention and that the teacher believes in the student's learning potential.

during this time. It's a writing conference, but it's focused on their constructed responses."

The teacher offered that he had developed any number of checklists and rubrics, but his students didn't seem to use them all that often. "I'm really focusing on self-regulation skills this semester. I want them to get more skilled at using these tools so they can measure their own progress toward goals." Mr. Zhang uses his daily purpose statements as a way for students to link what they are doing with what they are learning. "Those [purpose statements] really help for keeping them on track—and keeping me on track, too. They remind me to target my feedback so that it aligns with the goals."

Know How to Develop Success Criteria

Mr. Zhang's emphasis on feedback about self-regulatory behaviors is consistent with the fourth assumption about teacher clarity: that teachers and students understand what success looks like. Eighty-six percent of students report that they want to do their best at school, but in focus groups we often hear students express a need for increased clarity regarding expected outcomes. "I am just not sure what my teacher wants from me." "It is so hard to have seven different teachers and all of them expect different things." And one of our personal favorite responses, "Trying to get an A is like peeing in the wind . . . you just go for it and hope for the best."

> 86% of students report that they want to do their best at school, but in focus groups we often hear students express a need for increased clarity regarding expected outcomes.

Feedback is the effort to close the gap between current performance and desired outcomes. But feedback is far less effective when students are not clear on what those desired outcomes are. Termed *success criteria*, desired outcomes are concrete and demonstrable and are used by students to set goals and monitor their progress. Student goal setting is a powerful means for increasing student achievement; with an effect size of 1.44, it triples the speed of student learning (Hattie, 2012). It is heartening to hear that 85% of the high school students in the Student Voice database report that "getting good grades is important to me." But grades alone serve as poor success criteria, and in fact they can interfere with student goal setting.

There's a difference between "I want to get an *A* in Math" and "I want to get really good at factoring polynomials because chemistry requires it." The first is a performance goal, which has its limitations because its focus is on demonstrating competence to others, rather than learning. Under the worst of circumstances, a focus on performance goals is associated with cheating (Midgley, Kaplan, & Middleton, 2001). The second is a mastery goal, in which the student's focus is on the acquisition of a skill or set of knowledge. To use another example, it's the difference between passing a world language course and actually learning how to speak a new language. Schools are predicated on grades as performance goals, but grades are best augmented by mastery goals that spotlight the learning.

Mastery goals should not be so lofty that they are seen as nearly unattainable for students. To be able to explain the role of incentives and scarcity in a market economy is too distant a goal for a third-grade student and not of much use to her. However, a mastery goal of being able to explain concepts of scarcity in the story *The Hard-Times Jar* (Smothers, 2003) is attainable. Teachers of younger children often rely on "I can" statements to make mastery goals more concrete for students. Therefore, "I can explain how scarcity affects Emma's decisions" is a student-friendly version of success criteria.

Teachers share success criteria with students through

- Exemplars
- Modeling
- Negotiation

Eighth-grade science teacher Jeremy Hopkinson keeps *exemplars* gathered from previous years to show his students how lab reports are constructed. "I make sure to show them a range of quality, so they can see what constitutes successful and less than successful lab reports," he said. His grade-level colleague Monique Obonyo uses anchor papers identified by her state department of education for her English students.

A second method is *modeling and demonstrating* how you as a teacher make decisions about quality. Kindergarten teacher Linda Jamison used

> Feedback is the effort to close the gap between current performance and desired outcomes. But feedback is far less effective when students are not clear on what those desired outcomes are.

Video 9
The Importance of Success Criteria

resources.corwin.com/ engagementbydesign

samples illustrating stages of writing development that were in her commercial language arts program to make a large developmental writing continuum, and she displayed it at eye level for her students to use. "I meet with students during our conferences and we look at the 'writing wall' together," she said. "With my help, the children place themselves on the writing continuum, and then we talk about their next goal. Right now I've got a number of them who are paying attention to the space they leave between words."

The third method, *negotiation,* is useful when you want to develop success criteria in partnership with students. Ninth-grade students in Walt Connelly's science class developed success criteria for designing an automatic dog feeder. Mr. Connelly collaborated with the class to develop agreed-on indicators of a successful project: consistent amount and timing of feedings, easy for the dog to operate, a storage system to keep the food fresh, sturdy enough to withstand a pet's physical contact, and a cost of no more than $25.00 in materials. "This gave them a way to begin considering what qualities would make for a good automatic dog feeder, rather than me just doing the thinking for them. The only item I specified was the budget because that's how much they're allocated," the teacher explained. "But the 30 minutes or so that we took to develop this success criteria at the onset of the project was well worth it because it got their wheels turning."

> 85% of the high school students in the Student Voice database report that "getting good grades is important to me." But grades alone serve as poor success criteria, and in fact they can interfere with student goal setting.

Rubrics and Checklists

The examples of success criteria in the previous section fall into two categories: rubrics and checklists. These are tangible items that students can reference as they measure their progress toward goals. Rubrics can be either holistic or analytic, and they may be task specific or general. A holistic writing rubric will provide a point scale, often four points, with each level describing the overall quality. Holistic rubrics are used more often for large-scale assessments, as their drawback is that they do not provide specific feedback to the learner. They can be difficult to use for assessment purposes, especially when the characteristics of a student's work span more than one category. Figure 3.3 has an example of a holistic rubric.

HOLISTIC ARGUMENTATIVE WRITING RUBRIC

4 **Advanced**	Essay has a clear focus, with multiple supporting details aligned to each claim. Each claim is logical and is consistent with the overall purpose. There are few or no spelling or grammar errors that interfere with meaning.
3 **Proficient**	Essay has a focus, and there is at least one supporting detail for each claim. The argument is logical but lacks some transitions or enumerations to support the reader's understanding. There are few or no spelling or grammar errors that interfere with meaning.
2 **Developing**	The purpose is somewhat unclear and is left to the reader to infer. There is a least one supporting detail for each claim. There is a logical order to the information, but there are few enumerations or transitions. Some spelling or grammatical errors interfere with meaning and clarity.
1 **Needs Improvement**	The purpose is unclear, and the logic of the claims is disorganized. Some claims do not have supporting details. The number of spelling or grammar errors significantly interferes with meaning and clarity.

Figure 3.3

Available for download at **resources.corwin.com/engagementbydesign**

Most classroom rubrics are analytic; they allow for a deeper look at specific criteria. These rubrics are more useful for feedback, especially formative assessment, as they provide the teacher and student with means for discussing elements that are meeting expectations and the next steps for improvement. An example of an analytic rubric appears in Figure 3.4. This citizenship rubric is used at the middle and high school where three of us work. This rubric provides the student, teacher, and sometimes the family with a shared understanding of the social and behavioral expectations of a successful student. We encourage students to use rubrics for academic and nonacademic purposes to regularly self-assess their progress toward goals. For example, a writing rubric takes on far more meaning for a student when she is asked to score it herself and attach it to a draft. This gives the teacher insight into how that student's perception of her status and progress align with the teacher's expectations.

Checklists offer a simpler format for a student to ensure that she has included all the elements of a project or assignment. Checklists can be task specific, as was the one developed by Mr. Connelly and his class for the automatic dog feeder. Because these are a yes/no format, the feedback about the quality of an item is less apparent, although it can signal to the learner when something has been omitted or is of an insufficient quantity. Again, these are best used by students first, as they build self-regulatory habits such as reviewing work and comparing it to criteria.

Video 10
Feedback

resources.corwin.com/ engagementbydesign

Formative Evaluation

Purpose statements, feedback, and success criteria are contributory components to a formative evaluation system. Although sometimes narrowly understood as benchmarks or interim assessments that happen two or three times a year, formative evaluation occurs with much greater frequency, often daily. Daily purpose statements and exit slips or other end-of-lesson reflections, like the minute notes Ms. Lockwood uses to bracket each lesson, provide information that teachers can use to plan "next steps" lessons. Formative feedback, both verbal and written, moves students forward throughout the lesson as they approach success. The methods used to check for understanding throughout include noticing student cognition and responding with questions, prompts, and cues, a hallmark of an expert teacher (Jacobs et al., 2010).

CITIZENSHIP RUBRIC

To receive a score, the student meets several, but not necessarily all, of the following criteria:

	Excellent	Good	Needs Improvement	Unacceptable
Welcome	Responds positively to and takes action on feedback.	Responds positively to feedback and frequently takes action on it.	Inconsistently responds to and takes action on feedback.	Regularly struggles with feedback and/or fails to take action on the feedback given.
	Demonstrates and models leadership qualities in the community (e.g., verbal and nonverbal communication is welcoming; encourages others to be welcoming; mentors others to foster a welcoming environment).	Demonstrates a welcoming attitude toward others (verbal and nonverbal).	Welcoming attitude is demonstrated at times (e.g., verbal and/or nonverbal communication is at times less welcoming).	Makes others feel unwelcome. Refuses to help others when requested; disrupts others and/or the learning environment.
	Actively seeks out interaction with adults.	Interacts with adults regularly and occasionally initiates contact.	Interacts with adults positively when approached, but rarely initiates contact.	Avoids contact with adults.
Do No Harm	Demonstrates concern for others and the learning environment and models leadership qualities that improve circumstances.	Demonstrates concern for others and the learning environment and follows the lead of others to improve circumstances.	Often demonstrates concern for others and the learning environment.	Repeatedly does physical, verbal, or emotional harm to others and/or the learning environment.
	Consistently and actively participates in, and at times leads, the restorative process (circles, conferences, etc.). The contributions are insightful and advance the discussion. Seeks adult assistance and intervention to prevent harm.	Consistently and willingly participates in and contributes meaningful ideas to the restorative process (circles, conferences, etc.).	Participates in the restorative process (circles, conferences, etc.).	Significant disruption to the community resulting in harm (restoring harm to those hurt can result in change in citizenship). Rarely or unwillingly participates in the restorative process (circles, conferences, etc.).

Figure 3.4

	Excellent	Good	Needs Improvement	Unacceptable
Do Not Harm (continued)	Consistently presents own work in class and encourages academic honesty in the learning community (e.g., does not allow others to copy his or her work, counsels others to make ethical academic decisions).	Consistently presents own work in class and contributes to an ethical learning environment (e.g., does not allow others to copy his or her work).	Inconsistently presents own work in class and occasionally contributes to an ethical learning environment (e.g., does not allow others to copy his or her work).	Submits plagiarized or copied work in class and/or allows others to copy his or her work.
	Consistently follows courtesy policy in regard to use of personal electronic devices and anticipates when and how these PEDs are best used.	Consistently follows teacher directions regarding use of personal electronic devices.	Occasionally needs reminders or redirection regarding the use of personal electronic devices.	Repeatedly uses personal electronic devices despite teacher reminder and redirection.
Choice Words	Consistently influences others by modeling positive and appropriate language.	Often models positive and appropriate language.	Demonstrates understanding of appropriate and kind language and strives to use it.	Frequently uses language that degrades or belittles self or others.
	Consistently communicates kindly with peers both in and out of the classroom. Consistently uses academic language to express ideas in class discussions.	Often communicates kindly with peers both in and out of the classroom. Strives to use academic language to express ideas in class discussions.	Occasionally uses language that degrades or belittles self or others, or is inappropriate for school, but understands its effects and consequences.	Regularly uses inappropriate language (language that is not well-suited for school or academic settings). Remains unaware of or resistant to the effects and consequences of harsh language despite adult guidance.
Never Too Late to Learn	In attendance 95% or more of the time. Sets a scholarly example through careful preparation for learning (e.g., completing assignments, anticipating topics, bringing additional	In attendance 95% or more of the time. Comes to class on time and prepared intellectually and organizationally to learn (e.g., completed assignments, materials,	In attendance 95% or more of the time. Usually comes to class on time and prepared to learn (e.g., completed assignments, materials, completed	In attendance < 95% of the time. Often unprepared to learn without assignments completed. Often out of class for prolonged periods of time, negatively impacting

(Continued)

	Excellent	Good	Needs Improvement	Unacceptable
Never Too Late to Learn (continued)	materials to contribute to class discussion).	completed out-of-class readings for discussion).	out-of-class readings for discussion).	his or her individual learning and that of the group.
	Reliably present throughout class and makes decisions to minimize impact of brief time out of class.	Frequently present throughout class and often makes decisions to minimize impact of brief time out of class.	Usually present throughout class, although impact of time out of class is sometimes prolonged and requires teacher redirection.	Attitudes and/or contributions are counterproductive to the group and the learning environment.
	Constructive in groups as a member, regularly serving as a leader and promoting and supporting the leadership of others.	Constructive in groups, sometimes as a leader and consistently as a member.	Constructive in groups as a member.	Routinely inattentive to class discussions; rarely participates; often offers information that is off topic.
	Can be relied upon to contribute to discussions to advance the learning of self and others by posing questions and making connections to other disciplines and subjects.	Frequently contributes to class discussions in ways that advance the learning of self and others, occasionally posing questions or making connections to other disciplines and subjects.	Often contributes pertinent and on-topic information to class discussions.	Avoids accepting challenges. Needs to be reminded to get help when needed. Gives up easily. Does not take advantage of help offered.
	Reliably seeks resources or academic assistance independently in order to persevere (additional materials, academic recovery, tutoring, intervention, office hours, homework completion, etc.).	Frequently seeks resources or academic assistance with little or no prompting, in order to persevere (additional materials, academic recovery, tutoring, intervention, office hours, homework completion, etc.).	Needs prompting and encouragement to seek resources or academic assistance in order to persevere (additional materials, academic recovery, tutoring, intervention, office hours, etc.).	Needs continuous redirection and/or attention. Routinely needs to be reminded to put non-classroom materials away and return to a learning state.

online resources

Available for download at **resources.corwin.com/engagementbydesign**

Ongoing formative evaluation is essential for teacher clarity. The responses, insights, and behaviors of students should rightly be seen as feedback *to* the teacher. It is difficult to imagine how a teacher would be able to adjust the pacing, content, and instruction of a unit of study without closely observing how students are responding. Formative assessment practices and pedagogical content knowledge have a reciprocal relationship (Falk, 2012). In other words, teachers simultaneously build and utilize formative assessments and pedagogical content knowledge to strengthen both.

> Formative evaluation occurs with great frequency, often daily.

Importantly, this information is then used to guide the next learning expectation. It's a never-ending cycle, with teachers identifying gaps in students' knowledge and performance, establishing learning expectations, designing lessons and tasks, monitoring success, providing feedback, and then taking action based on the results. Unfortunately, in too many classrooms, there are gaps in this system. And when there are gaps in teacher clarity, student learning suffers.

Conclusion

The intersection between the teacher and the content is an important consideration in student engagement. As we noted in the previous chapter, relationships are critical for students' learning. In this chapter, we focused on the value of teacher clarity. Both are important for students to learn. But the four components of teacher clarity are not always in sync. In some places, teachers do not know what students need to learn, either because they don't know their students' strengths very well or because they don't understand the standards. In other places, teachers need to focus on the evidence regarding how people learn. In still other places, teachers need to communicate the learning expectations to students so that they share in the responsibility for their learning. And finally, in some places, success is not clearly defined for teachers or for students, and they trudge along assuming that the tasks they complete will result in successful learning. These four aspects of teacher clarity deserve attention and are fairly easy to implement. In the next chapter, we focus our attention on the third piece of low-hanging fruit: challenge. As we have noted before, taken together, relationships, clarity, and challenge create engagement in students and teachers that results in better learning for everyone.

CHALLENGE

The students in Kristin Williams's class were engaged in a conversation about naming buildings, especially schools, after former slave owners. The class had read a number of articles, pro and con, about changing the names of buildings. In some articles, authors argued that changing the names would send a message about the atrocities that these people committed. Others argued that the historical figures lived in a different context and that they did other things in their lives to earn their place in history. As Ms. Williams said, *"There is no right answer to this question. We are not having a debate and trying to make a decision. We're trying to understand the perspective of different people and then come to a personal decision about our respective beliefs. Given that we've read so much and talked about individual articles already, today will be an opportunity for us to engage in a Socratic seminar to exchange ideas."*

A Socratic seminar is

> a formal discussion, based on a text, in which the leader asks open-ended questions. Within the context of the discussion, students listen closely to the comments of others, thinking critically for themselves, and articulate their own thoughts and their responses to the thoughts of others. They learn to work cooperatively and to question intelligently and civilly. (Israel, 2002, p. 89)

A good Socratic seminar provides students an opportunity to ask questions to probe deeper, clarify their own understandings, paraphrase and add, and synthesize a variety of different views. The seminar starts with a key question that the leader (who can be the teacher or a student) asks. The discussion continues without students raising their hand to talk. Students practice active listening skills such as nodding, making eye contact, leaning forward, providing feedback, and listening carefully to others. A key to the conversation is the continued reference to the text(s) as students provide evidence and examples to support their responses. Ms. Williams adds a technology component to her Socratic seminar. "We always have an inside circle of students who are engaged in active discussion and an outside circle of observers who are taking notes. I added a backchannel so that the outside circle students are seeing the thinking of one another in real time." In this case, Ms. Williams's backchannel is a discussion board on the learning management system. At the end of the Socratic seminar, students read each other's virtual comments and individually summarize the content of the discussion as they try to capture their new understandings of the text(s). Common prompts for the summary phase include the following:

- Based on this seminar, what are the most important points about this text or texts?
- How did my understanding of the text(s) change?
- What concepts do I understand now that I didn't understand before the seminar?
- The main ideas I've taken away from the text(s) and seminar are. . . .
- What areas are still unresolved for me, and in which areas have I reached clarity?

At one point in the discussion about naming buildings after former slave owners, Marlo commented, *"The president of Harvard said, 'The people and culture behind these names and titles should be historically understood and contextualized.' I'm starting to agree with that because if we change all of the names, then maybe no one will learn about these people and the good and bad that they did."* (See Duehren & Thompson, 2016.)

Anthony responded, *"This is hard! I'm not sure what I think right now. Starting the seminar, I wanted to change all of the names. Now I'm not so sure. Does anyone have a strong reason for changing the names?"*

Yes, it is hard, and it should be. When students interact with content, it's supposed to be challenging. If they already know how to do all of the things that they are asked to do at school, then we're wasting their time. Appropriate levels of challenge are an inherent part of the engagement by design process. Challenging content and tasks stretch student thinking and help them understand their own growing capacity for learning. As we noted in Chapter 1, challenge has a powerful impact on students' learning, but we have to learn to welcome the struggle.

If students already know how to do all of the things that they are asked to do at school, then we're wasting their time.

Inviting the Struggle

We cannot count the number of times in the past couple of years that teachers have told us that they don't want their students to struggle. One teacher said, "If my students are struggling, then I'm not doing my job." Another said, "It makes me uncomfortable to see my students struggle. That's what scaffolding is for, so that they don't struggle." A third teacher said, "I really don't even like the word *struggle*. I want reading to be easy for them." Despite the focus on "rigor," it seems that there is an anti-struggle mentality in many schools. As educators, we have to increase the challenge that students experience in school. This can be a difficult approach for students to accept ("I've always been an A student") and for their parents, too, who may witness their child struggling and wonder whether there's something wrong. That's why we reserve struggle for the classroom, in the presence of an adult who knows how to leverage it for learning. We'll provide a rationale for the recommendation of struggle as part of the learning process and then turn our attention to the types of tasks that ensure appropriate levels of challenge.

Perhaps the most obvious theoretical support for struggle comes from Vygotsky (1978) and his Zone of Proximal Development. As he noted, there is a difference between what a learner can accomplish alone versus in the presence of a more capable other. It's not as simple as noting what a learner can and cannot do because there is a grey area between the dichotomy: *what a learner can do with support*. Importantly, Vygotsky observed that children were able to independently complete more complex tasks after they had received help from others. If students are only presented with texts and tasks that they can already read and complete on their own, then there is no need for a more capable other and there are limited possibilities for additional learning.

Even more support comes from Kapur's research on productive failure (e.g., Kapur, 2008), which suggests that the more a student struggles, and even fails, while trying to learn new information, the more likely that student is able to recall and apply that information later. As Kapur (2014) noted,

Video 11
Challenge

*resources.corwin.com/
engagementbydesign*

Learning from mistakes, errors, and failure seems intuitive and compelling. Everyone can relate to it. But if failure is a powerful learning mechanism, why do we wait for it to happen? Why can't we design for it, understand how and when it works? What if designing for failure while learning a new concept or skill could result in more robust learning? (para. 1)

At least according to these perspectives, students should be challenged—and should even struggle—on a regular basis. Additionally, 43% of students tell us they like challenging assignments, and 81% report pushing themselves to do better academically. We are vested in seeing both of these statistics increase. To accomplish this, teachers have to balance the difficulty and complexity of the tasks they assign. We think of difficulty as the amount of work, time, or effort that the learner has to exert. And we think of complexity as the type of thinking, the number of steps, or the necessary background knowledge required of the task. These two concepts, difficulty and complexity, are placed on different axes, creating four quadrants (see Figure 4.1).

In the lower left-hand quadrant, tasks are of low difficulty and low complexity. This is the *fluency* quadrant. We don't just mean how fast someone reads, but rather the procedural and conceptual fluency with which tasks are completed. As we will describe in greater detail later, this is the way in which students develop automaticity. And automaticity is the goal of all of our efforts. Over time, and with practice, things should become automatic for students. When automaticity is reached, students no longer have to use their working memory to accomplish tasks. Instead, their working memory is freed to focus on problem solving and reflection. Consider a reading comprehension example. At some point, students are introduced to synthesizing information. At first, they have no idea what this means. It is likely that their teacher will model for them. Then students will practice, laboriously at first, until they can synthesize information with conscious effort. With more and more practice, synthesizing becomes a habit that they do as they read. Eventually, synthesizing is automatic and only needs to be thought

43% of students say they like challenging assignments, and 81% report pushing themselves to do better academically.

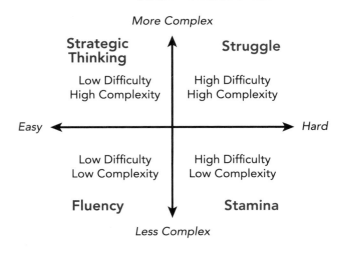

Figure 4.1

about when the text is really complicated or dense. Otherwise, synthesizing simply occurs as part of the overall fluent experience that students have.

In the bottom lower right quadrant, difficulty has increased but complexity remains low. We think of this as the *stamina* quadrant. Tasks in this quadrant require perseverance, determination, and grit. Students have to remain focused and work to complete these types of tasks. Some people criticize tasks in this quadrant as "low level," but when asked about their students' ability to work independently versus giving up when the going gets hard, they realize that this is an important area of challenge for many students. Stamina is an important aspect of learning and is one of the indicators of mindset that we have discussed previously (Dweck, 2006). Students with a fixed mindset tend to give up when they experience frustration or failure and don't seem to be able to rally resources to continue working through the situation. To build a growth mindset, students need to experience challenging tasks that require their stamina, *and* they need to hear from valued adults that their efforts are worthy and valuable and appreciated.

Tasks that fall below the horizontal (easy to hard) line can often be completed individually and independently. Teachers and parents can create tasks, assignments, and activities for children and youth to do by themselves that build their fluency and stamina. For example, sight word recognition for young children is a fluency activity. One of our friends has a preschooler who wants to read. He asks her all of the time what the words on the page say. To help him, she has listed more than 100 sight words on index cards. As he reads them, he gets to keep the cards he knows, and she keeps the cards he does not yet know. Over the course of a couple of months, he mastered all of the cards and still likes to play the game to show that he can win all of the cards. Our friend continues to add new words to the stack as his reading skills progress.

Wide, independent reading is one task that can provide students with stamina practice. At the kindergarten level, silent sustained reading isn't very silent and rarely is sustained. Instead, students talk about their books and ask questions of others. As their stamina increases, students can read independently for longer and longer amounts of time. And as Ivey and Broaddus (2001) noted, students really enjoy having time to read. But this requires that teachers or parents provide access to worthy texts, encourage students to read for longer and longer amounts of time, and create an environment that values reading.

These two examples of fluency and stamina come from the world of literacy, but every discipline has tasks that mirror them. Students learn math facts, the periodic table of elements, and how to determine sources when analyzing an historical document. Our point here is that tasks below the easy-to-hard line can be completed individually, whereas tasks above the line more frequently require collaboration with others.

The upper left-hand quadrant, in which complexity increases but difficulty does not, requires that students engage in *strategic thinking*. They have to slow down and focus because even though there may not be much difficulty, the task is complex. For example, while reading a dense piece of informational text in social studies, students may realize that the author has provided a great deal of information and that they should take notes for later. That's a strategic thought. Similarly, when the teacher assigns a multi-step extended project, students should learn to ask themselves whether they are on the right track, whether their efforts meet the success criteria, whether they are likely to meet the deadline, and whether each member of the group has an opportunity to contribute. These are also strategic thoughts.

We think of the final quadrant, the upper right side, as the *struggle* quadrant. Tasks in this quadrant are both complex and difficult. They are time consuming and require deeper thinking. For example, when students read multiple documents in a science class and then have to present their findings, they are likely engaged in a task that requires expertise. These tasks demand mastery of basic skills and competency in content knowledge. Students are expected to apply their knowledge and skills in unique ways to solve complex problems in this quadrant. As an example, rich mathematical tasks usually fall into this quadrant. These tasks typically have multiple ways to reach a solution, require trial and error, and have the potential to reveal patterns or lead to generalizations or unexpected results. They are not easy to solve, but they are interesting, and students tend to find them worth their time.

In the sections that follow, we explore each of the quadrants in greater detail:

- Fluency
- Stamina
- Strategic thinking
- Struggle that builds expertise

Before we pursue challenge, a low-hanging piece of fruit, it is instructive to note once again that the goal is fluency, habit building, or automaticity. In other words, the tasks that students are assigned should eventually become part of them and their routines. For example, having to stop to make a prediction or estimate an answer should eventually become an automatic habit that students use. When it happens, we can say that the student has transferred learning. And transfer of learning is our collective goal. As Wiggins and McTighe (2011) noted, "The ability to

transfer is arguably the long-term aim of all education. You truly understand and excel when you can take what you have learned in one way
or context and use it in another, on your own" (p. 14).

Fluency

A mark of any expert is the ability to perform acts with a level of fluidity, speed, and accuracy. Underlying any complex action is a host of
subskills that make it possible to perform at high levels. Think of the
mechanics of an Olympic runner's stride or a medical diagnostic specialist who accurately identifies an obscure disease as a patient's ailment.
In both cases, they rely on the ability to perform a task without hesitation, with high degrees of accuracy, and with speed. Fluent skills are an
important factor in the development of expertise.

> The goal is fluency, habit building, or automaticity. The tasks that students are assigned should eventually become part of them and their routines.

In education, fluency is primarily considered in terms of rapid recognition of specific skills, especially in reading, writing, and mathematics. In
reading, automaticity, which is the ability to subconsciously recognize
letters and words, is known to contribute to fluent reading (LaBerge &
Samuels, 1974). Closely related is reading fluency, which describes the
rate, accuracy, and prosody present in oral and silent reading, which
further contributes to comprehension (Samuels, 1979). Writing fluency
includes a child's ability to rapidly and accurately form letters, spell
words, and transform thoughts into logically arranged sentences and
paragraphs (Berninger & Swanson, 1994). Mathematical fluency is tied
closely to mastery of computational facts (Gagne, 1967). Performance of
discrete skills should not be confused with reading, writing, and mathematical knowledge. However, disfluent performance of discrete skills is
an impediment to high levels of learning.

More broadly speaking, fluency should not be narrowly viewed as
something of interest only to those teaching young children. In fact,
throughout our lifetimes we are continually moving toward more fluent
production. Older readers are able to read increasingly complex texts
while maintaining comprehension, and older writers are able to tailor
purpose, audience, and genre to meet their needs. Older mathematicians
become increasingly adept at leveraging a variety of problem-solving

procedures and formal reasoning to complete rich tasks. Likewise, factual and procedural knowledge in other disciplines over time increasingly becomes an issue of fluency, rather than strategic thinking. Whether teaching young children discrete skills or older students how to activate factual, conceptual, or procedural knowledge with little hesitation, it is useful to understand three tools that can build fluency:

> Underlying any complex action is a host of subskills that make it possible to perform at high levels.

- Spaced practice
- Repeated reading
- Mnemonics

Of course, there are others. In this chapter, we'll focus on these three.

Spaced Practice

We have all made the mistake sometime in our academic careers of trying to pull an all-nighter to cram for a test the following day. In addition to making ourselves utterly miserable, we undoubtedly figured out that this wasn't an especially effective strategy. Mass practice, that is, increasing the number of rehearsals within a short time span, is not useful in most cognitive tasks. Far more effective is spaced practice, in which rehearsals are distributed regularly over a longer time period. In fact, spaced practice has an effect size of 0.71 (Hattie, 2009), making it a very useful approach for students' learning. This has implications for the study skills we teach to students, such as regularly reviewing and summarizing notes, rereading more challenging portions of the textbook, talking with other people about the content, and asking questions to check for understanding. To be sure, adolescents are somewhat resistant to this information, so it can be useful to show students how you apply it in your own teaching.

For example, French teacher Michael Graydon reminds his students about how he introduces and reinforces new vocabulary terms in each unit. "Three times a week I have them review new vocabulary with partners for 10 minutes," he explained. "But during the first unit, I had them study additional terms during class for a 30-minute session. After they took the test the following week on both sets of vocabulary words, I shared the results with them. They get to see that they did much better on the terms they studied three times for the 10-minute sessions, compared to those they only studied once for 30 minutes," explained Mr. Graydon. "It was an eye-opener for them to understand that it's not just about time but about how you space the time you have."

First-grade teacher Audra Valentine has enacted the principle of spaced practice in her calendar math routine she uses each morning. "It's part of the circle we start each day with," she said. Each day she reviews the date and the class calculates the number of days they have been in school. But the emphasis is on number sense, "skip counting," and mental math. "We have a number of chants to rehearse ways to count by 2s, 3s, and so on, and we further represent these with Cuisenaire rods and unifix cubes. Every day we do some mental math to figure out a problem that applies to the class," said Ms. Valentine. "Today I've got 10 oranges to share with 20 students at snack time, so we'll need to figure out how to do that." This daily routine takes about 10 minutes, but it provides her students with regular opportunities to practice their number sense and number facts.

Repeated Reading

Rereading text increases the reader's understanding of the text and contributes to increased accuracy and rate. It's likely you've experienced a similar phenomenon as a teacher. You're teaching your class when a student worker from the front office comes into your classroom and hands you a note to read to your students. If you didn't read it silently to yourself first, you probably stumbled over some words and used incorrect inflection, which jumbled up the message. Taking just a few moments to read it to yourself before reading it aloud would have helped. That's why cold readings of text don't work. So-called "popcorn reading" or "round robin reading," where students take turns reading passages from the textbook aloud to the class, not only are painful to listen to, but also actually interfere with the comprehension of the reader as well as of the listeners.

Repeated reading of text deepens comprehension and contributes to increasingly fluent reading (Samuels, 1979). Not all text needs to be reread more than once, but those that are more complex should. Unfortunately, we often see repeated reading relegated to isolated skill instruction, where the intention is simply to increase a student's oral reading fluency. We argue that giving students regular opportunities to reread, especially to gain content knowledge, builds sound habits. Kindergarten teacher Ofelia Madera models the habit of rereading during interactive read alouds. She will pause after an important passage in the story, saying, "I want to read that paragraph again. A lot just happened in our story, and I want to make sure I understand it." Third-grade teacher Trevor Kendrick has his students regularly engage in partner reading to build fluency while building knowledge. Partner reading requires that two students have the same text and read it several times to one another. The stronger reader goes first, while his partner follows along silently in the text. Then the roles shift, and the second student reads the same passage again, this time aloud. "I don't explicitly name any of them as the 'stronger reader.' Instead, I just call them Partner A and Partner B," he explained. Importantly, he leverages knowledge building during his partner readings. "I don't have them read some random passage. I always choose something that is going to do double duty in building their background knowledge about a topic we're studying. We're learning about the Native Americans of our region in social studies right now, so this week's partner reading is about the Kickapoo tribe."

Mnemonics

Quick! What are the names of the five Great Lakes? If you answered Huron, Ontario, Michigan, Erie, and Superior by recalling HOMES, you used a mnemonic. Factual knowledge often falls into clusters, and these associated facts can be easier to recall using a mnemonic device—a memory technique to recall a related set of information. Depending on the discipline you teach, you may have introduced your students to similar name mnemonic devices: Roy G. Biv to recall the order and colors in visible light (red, orange, yellow, green, blue, indigo, and violet) or FANBOYS to recall the coordinating conjunctions in English (for, and, nor, but, or, yet, so).

The purpose of a mnemonic is to aid in information storage and retrieval. Although it is not a substitute for deep knowledge, mnemonics are useful in tying together a set of facts or concepts as a means of establishing schema. Mnemonics come in a variety of forms. Some are musical, for example. Most of us learned to recite the alphabet and the names of the 50 states by memorizing a song. No primary classroom would be complete without a repertoire of such songs. Another type of device is the expression mnemonic, such as recalling that "when two vowels go walking, the first one does the talking," or "I before E except after C." Even today, most of us as adults still silently run through the chant "30 days hath September" when figuring out how many days are in the current month.

As students progress developmentally, they expand their mnemonic capabilities. Frayer vocabulary cards use image mnemonics to assist students in recalling new terms (Frayer, Frederick, & Klausmeier, 1969). These are best constructed by the students themselves, so that the words and images take on greater meaning. A student-made vocabulary card for the word *noxious* appears in Figure 4.2. The upper left quadrant is used for the target vocabulary word, and the upper right quadrant contains a definition using the student's own words (not copied from the teacher). In this case, the student wrote "poisonous and deadly." Moving clockwise, the lower right quadrant is also student-generated, and it features a word or phrase that represents an opposite meaning, or a non-example: in this case, "harmless." Finally, the lower left quadrant is the student-generated image that represents the word's meaning visually.

A final kind of mnemonic device is the visual model, which organizes related information using a familiar shape representation.

Other graphic organizers perform a similar function. Sixth-grade science teacher Aminah Sabah teaches the hydrologic cycle using a cycle graphic organizer to show how water travels from land to sky and back. Seventh-grade English teacher Leann Harrington uses a similar graphic organizer to teach about the heroic cycle in literature. In both cases, the teachers are leveraging visually organized information to promote recall and initial understanding of terms and concepts. Although more teaching will follow, these visual models assist learners in linking concepts together to build a more complex schema.

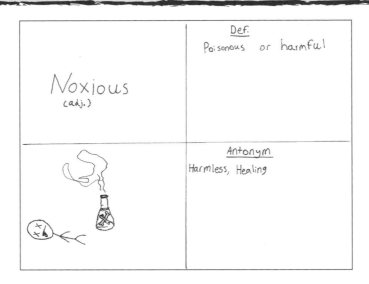

Figure 4.2

Practice

One of the commonalities you may have noticed in the classrooms profiled in the fluency section was practice. Practice does not make perfect, but it does make permanent, and that's what we're going for with tasks in the fluency quadrant. The goal is to ensure that students develop habits that they can mobilize and use independently, even beyond the walls of a given classroom. The reason practice works is based in the brain. Neural pathways are built, strengthened, and reinforced by use. These pathways become stronger and stronger the more often they are accessed. With practice, they become increasingly permanent and easier to mobilize.

We included fluency activities in the chapter on challenge for a couple of reasons. First, it's a challenge to get students to engage in the practice they need. Second, without sufficient practice and the transfer to automaticity, learning is always slowed, as students have to deliberately think about what to do next or what information they need. And third, for many students the tasks that are assigned in this quadrant are a challenge in and of themselves because students are not used to having to do these types of activities. Importantly, these are not the only activities students should complete. Their educational experience would be very limited if they only engaged in fluency-building tasks, but without these types of activities, students have a difficult time moving forward in the curriculum because they have failed to develop sufficient habits. In other words, students use their current habits in each of the other quadrants to accomplish tasks, and they develop new habits as they master tasks from other quadrants.

Stamina

Endurance. In it for the long haul. Staying power. Our society is filled with terms for stamina, especially when it comes to athletic endeavors. These catch phrases are important because lots of athletes want to quit before they have completed the task and they use these phrases to make it to the end. They muster the energy needed and the tenacity required to get the job done. Marathoners can't imagine ending their run at mile 25, with only 1.2 miles to go until the finish line. But that's what happens to a lot of students. Seventeen percent of students readily admit they give up when school work is hard. They just give up. They quit. They fail to complete the task. They do not persevere in the face of adversity.

For this very reason, teachers design tasks that build students' stamina. To take the marathon analogy a bit further, no trainer would ask a couch potato to run 26.2 miles on his first day of practice. Instead, she would develop a plan to build the stamina required to complete the task. She would also anticipate challenges, monitor for injuries, and ensure accountability, which metaphorically also happens in the classroom as students' stamina increases. Teachers understand the common misconceptions and probable errors that their students will make in learning content and then alert learners to those situations. They also monitor students' progress and provide feedback. Learning is much like developing athletic prowess: stamina is key.

> The goal is to ensure that students develop habits that they can mobilize and use independently, even beyond the walls of a given classroom.

Researchers who study persistence note that there are several things that teachers can do to help students develop stamina (e.g., Duckworth, 2016; Tough, 2012):

Marathoners can't imagine ending their run at mile 25, with only 1.2 miles to go until the finish line. But that's what happens to a lot of students.

- **Help learners understand and develop a growth mindset.** We have discussed growth mindsets elsewhere in the book, but students need to be taught about this so that they can monitor their own triggers. And the adults in their lives need to recognize effort as a valuable aspect of learning.

- **Push, but know when to stop.** The expectations have to be clear, and then when students want to quit, they need firm and gentle support from another person to keep going. Teachers should avoid telling students answers when they are wrong or when they are stuck. Rather, teachers should prompt and cue students toward the information. Importantly, students persist longer for teachers with whom they have great relationships. In essence, they don't want to disappoint, so they keep trying, often learning more in the process.

- **Model perseverance.** Far too many students lack an example of persistence. In fact, many students believe that learning comes easy for their teachers, and some think that their teachers already know everything. Young people need to see the adults in their lives persevere. They appreciate knowing that their teachers try, sometimes fail, and then try again.

- **Teach positive self-talk.** As the saying goes, it's really about mind over matter. We all give up when we start to tell ourselves that we can't do something anymore. In reality, we probably can continue, but when self-talk becomes negative, we don't. We stop. We succumb to the inner dialogue of defeat. Instead, we have to engage in positive self-talk. Students have to learn how to use this type of inner speech to keep themselves motivated. Simply saying, *"I will read this one more time to figure out what the author is saying"* or *"I have done harder problems before; this one can't get me"* or *"I will stay with this at least five more minutes,"* can go a long way in building grit and stamina.

- **Remind them about their brains.** Most students have not heard of plasticity, the understanding that the brain changes based on how it is used. Reminding them that they get better and better at the tasks at hand by trying them and learning from their mistakes can serve as a powerful motivator for continued focus. Literally, the brain changes based on how it is used. Building stamina requires changes in the brain that simply don't occur from a single task. It's a much slower process, with slight increases in stamina each time the task requires a bit more.

In addition to these generic recommendations, there are specific instructional practices that teachers can use to build students' perseverance. In this chapter, we offer two sample tools for building stamina: wide independent reading and research projects. Having said that, it's important to note that these are just two examples. There are a wide range of tasks, assignments, or activities that can be used to increase stamina. Once again,

17% of students readily admit they give up when school work is hard.

it's important to note that the goal is fluency (automaticity). Challenging stamina-related tasks should become less difficult over time and eventually slide into the fluency quadrant. When that happens, we change up our stamina tasks and either increase the difficulty or change the type of information being used. For example, a group of ninth-graders were studying poetry. At first, they didn't like it much and complained rather bitterly about the selection of texts. They found the poems hard. As one student said, *"How do I know what a wheelbarrow stands for metaphorically? It's a wheelbarrow."* The unit required that students analyze numerous poems, none of which were that complex. Over time, students began to see patterns and recognize commonalities, and eventually poetry analysis was in their fluency range rather than a stamina task. At that point, the teacher could change genres, perhaps to dramas, increase the complexity of the poems selected, or perhaps select longer texts, each of which would have required additional stamina from the students. Now to the tools for developing stamina.

Wide Independent Reading

Earlier in this chapter, we briefly noted the value of wide independent reading in building students' stamina. At this point, we'll take the

Challenging,
stamina-related
tasks should
become less
difficult over time
and eventually
slide into the
fluency quadrant.

discussion a bit deeper. Wide reading builds students' background knowledge and their vocabulary (Mason, Stahl, Au, & Herman, 2003). It also builds stamina as students focus their energy on reading and not the latest video game or iPad app. They allow themselves to get lost in a book, whether narrative or informational text. And by *text*, we don't mean only the traditional printed book with chapters, but rather the range of texts we all read, including magazines, news articles, novels, informational texts, biographies, and so on. The key is to encourage students to focus long enough on a text so that they begin to think more deeply about the content.

When appropriate, provide students with the opportunity to make decisions about what to read. Less than half (44%) of students report having a voice in decision making at school, and only 58% believe they even possess the ability to make good decisions. Strategically guiding students how to make worthy choices of text for independent reading can be a good opportunity to teach decision-making skills and build student confidence to be leaders in their own learning.

Pilgreen's (2000) meta-analysis of wide reading noted a modest increase in reading achievement and a statistically significant effect on interest and motivation. She identified eight key factors for implementing an effective and efficient wide reading effort:

- **Access.** Students need to be flooded with reading materials. They need a wide range of topics and genres as well as text complexity levels.

- **Appeal.** Reading materials should be geared toward students' interests. Teachers can "bless" several books each day, noting the general topic of the text and the type of reader who might be interested in reading the text.

- **Conducive environment.** The setting should be quiet and comfortable. Wide reading should be relaxed yet focused, and the environment needs to communicate these expectations.

- **Encouragement.** Students need supportive adult role models for locating reading material. They also need reminders to focus on their reading and not other things and to talk about the texts they are reading.

- **Staff training.** It doesn't just happen; a school's staff should be well-versed in the goals and procedures of wide independent reading.

- **Nonaccountability.** Most controversially, Pilgreen found that students read more and had a more positive attitude when book reports were not required.

- **Follow-up activities.** Follow-up activities could include conversations about books read by students, or the teacher could encourage others to try them out. There are a number of different follow-up activities teachers can use, from book talks to book recommendations to golden lines ("the best line that I read today"), all of which enable students to share their reading with others.

- **Distributed time to read.** A common error is having one long period a week for wide reading. Pilgreen found that successful programs read 15–20 minutes daily.

Of course, reading should not be limited to the school day. Students should be reading outside of school, further developing their stamina. Students who read more get better, and those who don't read much fail to get better. And those who are more likely to read on their own are students who are already generally good readers. The opposite is true for weak readers. In describing this situation, Stanovich (1986) noted that the rich get richer and the poor get poorer. It's critical that teachers build students' stamina in wide reading across content areas, so that students build their stores of knowledge and thus are able to activate that knowledge while learning new content.

Research Projects

One of the stamina skills that students are expected to develop relates to independent research and informative essay writing. Students must be able to engage in research, which might be library research or a lab experiment, and then analyze, summarize, and synthesize findings in their own words. Typically, teachers provide a set of guidelines for students to use as well as a success criteria checklist so that students can monitor their progress. These types of projects begin in elementary school and continue through college and are assigned in many careers. Nancy's son is a mechanical engineer, and he writes these types of reports for his company on a regular basis.

In general, research projects are not complex. There is generally an agreed-upon topic and a framework that teachers provide for students. These projects are really about the planning and stamina required to complete the task. It's hard to produce a strong research paper in one sitting the night before it's due (even though we have all tried). This is why teachers typically assign research papers well in advance of the due date. We will consider two examples of research papers to highlight the role that stamina plays in completing this task.

44% of students report having a voice in decision making at school, and only 58% believe they even possess the ability to make good decisions.

The fifth graders in Carmen Valdez's class each identified a U.S. president whom they wanted to learn more about. Ms. Valdez provided students with a graphic organizer for their note taking as well as a template that they could download to use in writing their paper. In addition to the written essay, students had to submit a three-minute video to the class learning management system for others to view. Once all of the students had uploaded their videos, students would watch each other's videos and generate questions about different presidents and then vote to decide which one was the most influential president of all time. The tasks that came after the essay extended beyond stamina, but we thought you should know that students did not simply write informational reports in Ms. Valdez's class.

The students were provided library research time as well as drafting and editing time in class, but they had to monitor their own completion of the assignment. They could request a conference with their teacher or another student, and Ms. Valdez included milestones on a checklist for each student. For example, the first milestone included basic demographic information about the selected president such as birth and death date, spouse and children, locations lived, and major historical events during the presidency. Another milestone included five sources of information, four quotes from the president, three challenges the president faced during his term in office, two policies that positively impacted the American people, and one image of the president. By the end of the unit, students had to have submitted their essay addressing each of the required prompts.

Similarly, the tenth graders in Mike Stein's biology class were assigned a research project about genetic testing. As he said to his students,

> *Genetic testing is becoming more affordable and more accessible. Just think about how many people have already participated in efforts such as 23andme, including their genetic information in a large database. Your task, if you choose to accept it, which I know you will because it's a cool one, is to select any one of the more than 100 topics listed on our class webpage. Once you select it, it's yours, and no one else will be able to select it. You'll research the topic and write your report of at least 7 double-spaced pages with at least 10 references. You'll also present in groups that I will form to maximize controversy. Exciting, right?*

As in Ms. Valdez's class, students were provided some time to work on their research projects during class, but a lot of it was to be completed outside of class. Mr. Stein's school operates an extensive afterschool tutoring program. Mr. Stein contacted a local university to recruit biology students to serve as subject experts students could interview or share their ideas with. He put a lot of material on reserve in the school library so that students would experience immediate success in finding initial information for their projects. He also knew that students would have to continue searching beyond the information he provided to create strong papers.

Neither of these tasks was especially complex, but they did require stamina and dedication to complete the project. Students had to pace themselves, sustain their attention, and create cohesion in their work over several days. We are not suggesting that school be limited to independent projects that students complete alone but rather that some tasks demand increased stamina. You may have noticed a few keys that make independent stamina-focused tasks effective: choice, relevance, and differentiation.

Choice, Relevance, and Differentiation

Each of the examples we profiled in the area of stamina allowed students to exercise choice. In the area of wide reading, students were provided access to a wide range of texts. For the research projects, students had a choice of topic. *Choice* is important, as it serves as a motivator for students in completing these types of tasks, especially tasks that they complete individually. Yet only 60% of students report that their teachers encourage them to make decisions, a necessary skill for students to develop so they have the confidence to take action in learning and life.

> Only 60% of students report that their teachers encourage them to make decisions.

We are less worried about initial offerings of choice when students are working collaboratively because they are more likely to customize their group responses as they engage in the task. Limiting choice in stamina-related tasks increases the likelihood that students will give up before they have completed the assignment.

In addition to choice, *relevance* is an important consideration when students are faced with difficult tasks. How many of us have said (or heard students say) something like, "Why do I have to do these 15 problems? They take so long, and I am never going to use this information anyway." When the task is relevant, students are more likely to choose to complete it. For wide reading, finding texts that appeal to students, based on their interests, is important. Seventy-eight percent of students say they enjoy learning new things, but only 65% report having opportunities to learn new things that are interesting to them at school. By connecting text options to student interests, we can access the intrinsic curiosity students naturally possess for exploring the unknown.

Students should also be stretched so that their reading is comprehensive. For example, if a student only reads realistic fiction, the teacher may meet with the student and recommend a few books of a different genre but on the same topic. The first step may be to move from realistic fiction to historical fiction; jumping to poetry may be too far at this point. In the research examples, both teachers attempted to choose topics that allowed students to demonstrate mastery of content standards while also ensuring that the topics were current and relevant for students.

Finally, stamina tasks need to be *differentiated* to meet the diverse needs of students. In wide reading, there should be a range of texts available for students so that everyone is reading with a bit of difficulty but not so much as to require scaffolding from another person. In the research projects, the teachers provided checklists that students could use as well as a variety of instructional resources. The teachers were also monitoring students' success, ready to provide additional support as needed to ensure success.

> Limiting choice in stamina-related tasks increases the likelihood that students will give up before they have completed the assignment.

Building students' stamina is an important aspect of schooling. Students need to experience more difficult, but less complex, tasks that stretch their ability to focus and sustain an effort. Over time, they will learn to persevere and achieve. As Duckworth (2016) reminds us, "We want to believe that Mark Spitz was born to swim in a way that none of us were and that none of us could. We don't want to sit on the pool deck and watch him progress from amateur to expert. We prefer our excellence fully formed" (p. 39). The thing is, it takes time and persistence to achieve greatness.

Strategic Thinking

While fluency- and stamina-building tasks are largely completed independently, the strategic thinking quadrant represents a shift to an increasing number of interactions with the teacher and classmates. Strategic thinking has been defined in various ways, but include these abilities:

- Formulate goals and create a plan to achieve them
- Gather and integrate information

- Make decisions about how to proceed
- Reflect on one's actions and thinking
- Adjust actions based on these reflections

Many of these cognitive and metacognitive moves are refined in the company of others, especially through interactions designed to surface higher order thinking. The use of strategic thinking increases the rigor of the lesson, as students must consider multiple pathways rather than a single route to a solution. *Strategies* should be understood as different from *skills,* although both terms are often used interchangeably. In their discussion of the use of both terms in reading, Afflerbach, Pearson, and Paris (2008) make a distinction we feel is useful:

> Reading skills are automatic actions that result in decoding and comprehension with speed, efficiency, and fluency and usually occur without awareness of the components or control involved, while reading strategies are deliberate, goal-directed attempts to control and modify a reader's efforts to decode text, understand words, and construct meanings of text. Accomplished readers require a balance of both skills and strategies and the ability to shift seamlessly between the two when required. (p. 364)

We appreciate their definition, and we add that as children mature, some of these processes move from strategy to skill. However, students will not sufficiently learn how to enact their strategic thinking without a multitude of opportunities to do so. We'll address items from our bulleted list as an illustration. *Strategic thinking involves setting goals, making a plan, and making adjustments based on progress.* In the previous chapter, we devoted significant attention to the importance of setting purposes and success criteria. These practices are directly linked to goal setting, but without deliberative attention, children may not formulate goals. Seventy-eight percent of students believe it is important to set goals, and 80% report working hard to reach those goals. This is a good start, but *all* students need to understand the importance of setting goals and working hard to reach their goals. In too many cases, the opportunity and ability to set meaningful goals, and to reflect

78% of students believe it is important to set goals, and 80% report working hard to reach those goals.

on their progress and attainment, are missing. We find this is equally true for adult learners. Teacher Voice survey results show that 96% of teachers think it is important to set goals and that they work hard to reach their goals. However, only 66% believe that setting yearly goals with their supervisor is important to their work. Although the teachers and leaders we work with are accomplished and motivated, few will set goals for themselves unless they are given the time to compose them and discuss their intentions with others in a way that is meaningfully connected to their work.

In the section that follows, we will begin by discussing the importance of the following:

- Understanding how strategies are used to *resolve problems* through the process of reciprocal teaching

- The essential nature of *metacognition* and methods for promoting reflective thinking

- *Self-regulatory behaviors* that move strategic thinking forward to action

96% of teachers think it is important to set goals and that they work hard to reach their goals. However, only 66% believe that setting yearly goals with their supervisor is important.

Resolving Problems

Challenge lies in finding solutions to situations that are complex, yet developmentally appropriate. By that, we mean that we don't expect students to come up with an answer for solving climate change, curing cancer, or creating world peace, but we do want them to appreciate that what they are learning in school has relevance both in and out of the classroom.

Reciprocal teaching is a small group, text-based discussion protocol that promotes reading comprehension through attention to collaborative problem solving (Palincsar & Brown, 1984). Deemed one of the most effective tools for fostering comprehension in Grades 4 to 12, reciprocal teaching has been utilized for decades with informational texts in English, science, social studies, mathematics, and technical subjects. Hattie (2009) calculated an effect size of 0.74 for reciprocal teaching, making it the single most robust comprehension approach on his list of 195 effects. The format typically consists of four students who are reading and discussing an informational text that has been segmented into smaller passages (often one to three paragraphs), either in advance by the teacher or by group consensus. Each passage segment is read silently; then each member, who has an assigned function (Questioner, Clarifier, Summarizer, and Predictor) alternately leads and participates in a short discussion, co-constructing meaning as the group advances through the text. The process is repeated for each segment until the text is finished. This protocol contributes to students' knowledge of and ability to enact specific comprehension strategies in order to monitor and repair one's understanding.

All students need to understand the importance of setting goals and working hard to reach their goals.

Although designed originally for older students, modified reciprocal teaching protocols for younger children have emerged. Jenny Edwards uses a method described by Pratt and Urbanowski (2015) with her first-grade students. Ms. Edwards meets with small groups of students to read the beginning of a text aloud to them, stopping at key segments so that her students can discuss what has transpired. The teacher explains, "What I'm going after is their ability to monitor their understanding and make corrections when needed." Using two-sided cards labeled "click" (accompanied by a picture of a bicycle in motion) and "clunk" (with a picture of the bike with a flat tire), students label and identify when the teacher makes an error (the clunks). When the story makes sense, they hold up the "click" (Klingner & Vaughn, 1999). The students then read the remainder of the text, pausing at designated points to have a short discussion facilitated by the teacher. During this time, students are marking their own "clicks" and "clunks" so that the teacher can prompt self-correcting reading behaviors to repair meaning.

"I've seen an important difference this year since I've been doing this," said Ms. Edwards. "They're talking about how they're strategically repairing meaning with each other. It's great to hear a student say, 'Here's how I turned my clunk into a click.'"

Metacognition

The ability to notice one's own thinking, called metacognitive awareness, expands the positive effects established through strategic instruction. Although specific strategies, such as reviewing notes before a test, are useful, a student who is thinking metacognitively is also monitoring his progress, reflecting on his current level of understanding, and planning what other techniques he might need to use to master the material. In fact, metacognition is the ability to monitor, evaluate, and plan for one's own learning (Flavell, 1979). We've previously discussed the value of goal setting and opportunities for reflection (such as exit slips) to promote metacognition. But perhaps the best tool you have at your disposal is one that is itself metacognitive: the teacher think aloud.

Seventh-grade science teacher Cecily McNeill models metacognition as she thinks aloud with her students. During the introduction of an outdoor science lab her students would be completing the following day, she modeled her planning process:

> *My goal is to collect water samples from Miller's Pond, so I know I need to have my equipment prepared in advance for fieldwork. That means I've got to make sure I have all the items I need and that I'm able to transport them to the pond and back.*

The science teacher models making a list of the equipment she'll need, as well as reviewing the data collection sheet she'll take with her to record turbidity, temperature, oxygen levels, and acidity. *"I'm cross-checking the data I'll need to make sure I've got everything with me. If I don't do that, I'm more likely to leave something behind."* She thinks aloud, *"I'm not going to be of much help to myself if I don't keep my major scientific question in mind. The question I am trying to answer through my data analysis is, 'How healthy is Miller's Pond?' So now I'm asking myself, what other measures will I need to answer this question?"* She continues,

> *I'm realizing I can't fully answer this question if I don't also get a sense of the macroinvertebrates that are living in the pond. That's another measure of the pond's health. So if I'm also going to collect macroinvertebrates, I need to go back to my equipment list to add items.*

Ms. McNeill turns the planning over to the student teams, giving them the responsibility to prepare their own field kits for the outdoor lab. "I know I need to give them opportunities to figure out the planning and preparation needed for a big project like this. Scientific thinking requires a lot of reflective thought before, during, and after the lab. I don't want to have everything ready made for them. Scientists don't just buy a kit off a shelf. They design and plan their experiments and are always thinking reflectively about what's working and why."

Self-Regulation

A person's ability to utilize strategies as needed, monitor progress toward goals, and think metacognitively is crucial for self-regulatory academic behaviors, which is the coordination of all of these into action. Self-regulatory academic behaviors include preparation for work, seeking help when needed, and persistence in the face of difficulty. There is a developmental aspect to self-regulation, as younger children will not sustain these academic behaviors at the same level as older students, but even primary students are capable of acquiring and strengthening self-regulatory behaviors. If metacognition is thinking about one's thinking, then self-regulation is learning about one's learning.

Planning is an important self-regulatory skill. An important tenet of cooking is *mise en place*. Before beginning, the cook gets all the utensils, equipment, and ingredients set up. It minimizes all the running around, and if you don't have an important ingredient, you know before you've even begun and can problem-solve accordingly. Teach young students to plan for assignments by having them list and assemble the items they'll need, rather than always putting them on their tables for them. Older students should begin writing assignments with an outline so that they can gain a perspective for what they will be composing before they start. Many students use digital or paper calendars to record assignment due dates, but they would benefit from additional discussion about how one plans for work distribution during the week so that they are not faced with the last-minute scramble of starting a large assignment the night before it's due.

Challenge lies in finding solutions to situations that are complex, yet developmentally appropriate.

Help-seeking behaviors should also be taught and encouraged. Only 58% of students report feeling comfortable asking questions in class. Some students operate under the misconception that academically strong students operate independently and rarely ask for help. In truth, students with higher levels of academic self-regulation seek help and advice more often, with the intention of making themselves more autonomous, rather than only fixing an immediate problem (Ryan, Pintrich, & Midgley, 2001). It's the difference between "Can you fix this for me?" and "Can you fix this for me, and what can I do differently next time so it won't happen again?" Although we don't expect students to do this on their own, they can be prompted through your response. After addressing the issue, asking the student, *"What could you do differently next time?"* apprentices them into a view of errors as opportunities to learn. For many years, we have taught our own elementary and secondary students four questions about help to ask themselves each day, consistent with a helping curriculum described by Sapon-Shevin (2010):

> # Only 58% of students report feeling comfortable asking questions in class.

- Have I asked for help when I needed it?

- Have I offered help to someone else?

- Have I accepted help when offered by another?

- Have I politely declined help when I want to give it another try on my own?

In articulating and modeling help-seeking and help-giving behaviors, you are accomplishing several ends, including establishing a collegial learning community and strengthening social-emotional learning. Beyond their academic benefits, these are truly life skills they will draw on throughout their personal and professional lives.

Students use problem-solving and help-seeking behaviors to persevere in the face of challenge. These are factors in academic coping, and students who lack them are at risk for failure. In fact, one study found that the assessment of coping skills of ninth graders accurately predicted whether a student dropped out of high school or not (Hess & Copeland,

2001). Negative coping skills are associated with avoidance and include concealment, blaming others, and helplessness, while productive ones include recommitting to goals and seeking support (Skinner, Pitzer, & Steele, 2016).

Interestingly, in a study of 880 fourth to sixth graders, productive academic coping was directly linked to academic engagement (Skinner et al., 2016). In other words, students who were engaged were able to draw on this as a resource for persisting when faced with challenges and setbacks. We've all witnessed this countless times as we look at the faces of determined young people who play a sport, or an instrument, or a video game. They just refuse to give up, even when something isn't working. What do each of these situations have in common? A clear sense of what success looks or sounds like and a goal to achieve success. That's engagement, and that's exactly what we need in our classrooms, too. Although you may not be able to directly teach persistence and coping, you can certainly set the stage such that these elements—purpose, goals, opportunities to seek help, and so on—are present.

Struggle That Builds Expertise

Malcolm Gladwell's book *Outliers: The Story of Success* (2008) exposed the general public to the field of expertise development. Among the findings Gladwell shared were the effects of deliberative practice (10,000 hours). Although powerful, this timeline isn't achievable within the confines of a classroom. But 10,000 hours of practice isn't the only thing that contributes to expertise. Experts are able to formulate judgments about quality, make decisions, and evaluate situations with a high degree of accuracy. In school, capacity is built through tasks that require critical thinking skills. These critical thinking skills require that students recognize quality, are able to synthesize and analyze across sources, and can solve ill-defined or unstructured problems. In addition to posing content-related challenges, teachers need to create opportunities to work with students to solve problems outside of the classroom. Unfortunately, only 46% of students report having the opportunity to work with adults to find solutions to school problems. Students and teachers working together provide a powerful way to model a wide variety of critical thinking and problem-solving skills that students can apply to their learning and beyond. Other tasks that contribute to critical thinking development that also involve struggle include

- Peer critiques
- Close reading within and across documents
- Problem-based learning

Below, we will explore each in more detail.

Peer Critiques

Although most often associated with writing, peer critiques have grown in popularity in other disciplines, especially on projects and presentations. Some teachers are skeptical of peer critiques, as they may have concerns about accuracy. However, when students are taught to critique one another's work in constructive ways, the results can be very effective. In one study comparing teacher and student critiques, those done by peers were superior and focused on form, content, and message, while the teachers' feedback centered on error correction, rather than actionable feedback (Caulk, 1994).

The key is that they must be taught. Without guidance, peers will rely on instinctive techniques such as giving global praise ("This is great!") and word- and sentence-level editing (Simmons, 2003). However, students skilled at providing critiques are able to play back the text, thereby providing the writer with insight into how the draft is understood by a reader; pose questions that cause the writer to consider organizational changes; and provide specific suggestions for revision (Simmons, 2003). Figure 4.3 contains a chart of methods for teaching peer critiques to your students.

Fourth-grade teacher Victor Torres uses peer critiques as part of the Genius Hour program he hosts each week. Inspired by Google's leadership's commitment to provide time each week for employees to explore topics of their interest, Genius Hour has been applied in schools as

Only 46% of students report having the opportunity to work with adults to find solutions to school problems.

Video 12
Peer Critiques

*resources.corwin.com/
engagementbydesign*

TECHNIQUES TO TEACH PEER RESPONDING

Technique	What the Teacher Does	What Students Do
Sharing your writing	Shares a piece of writing and asks for response Shares rewrites tied to class response	Offer comments on the teacher's writing
Clarifying evaluation versus response	Shows evaluation is of product, while response is to writer	Understand that response is personable and helpful
Modeling specific praise	Shows how to tell what you like as a reader	Understand that cheerleading is too general to be helpful
Modeling understanding	Shows how to tell what you understood the piece to be about	Understand that reflecting back the piece to the writer is helpful
Modeling questions	Shows how to ask questions about what you didn't understand	Understand that questions related to the writer's purpose are helpful
Modeling suggestions	Shows how to suggest writing techniques	Understand that a responder leaves the writer knowing what to do next
Whole-class response	Moderates response by class to one classmate's piece	Offer response Hear the response of others Hear what the writer finds helpful
Partner response	Pairs up students in class to respond to pieces	Practice response learned in whole-class session
Comment review	Reads the comments of peers to writers Suggests better techniques Devises focus lessons	Get teacher feedback on comments
Response conference	Speaks individually with students who respond inappropriately	Have techniques reinforced

Source: Simmons, J. (2003). Responders are taught, not born. *Journal of Adolescent and Adult Literacy, 46,* p. 690.

Figure 4.3

time set aside weekly for students to investigate a topic, propose a project and timelines, and provide a deliverable. James, a student in Mr. Torres's class, was interested in learning more about how computer hacking is used to strengthen cybersecurity. He learned about hackathons and other competitions that are sponsored by organizations to expose weaknesses in their systems. James was most fascinated to learn about a second grader who is listed by Microsoft as one of its security researchers, after hacking his father's Xbox system to locate passwords. James's deliverable was a presentation to his class. As part of the development of his presentation, he met with Sofia, a classmate who served as peer responder. James had drafted his talk using presentation software, and he shared it with Sofia, who took notes throughout. When James was finished, she summarized the information so that James could listen to how it was understood. Sofia then posed clarifying questions and told James what she would like to know more about. James took notes during the critique and thanked Sofia when they were finished. When James presented to the class the following week, he credited Sofia as well. *"She asked me good questions so I could make it better,"* he said.

In one study of fourth to sixth graders, productive academic coping was directly linked to academic engagement.

Close Reading Within and Across Documents

Complex readings stretch the critical thinking skills of students. In other words, they cause students to appropriately struggle. Skilled readers are able to read closely in order to unearth the deeper nuances of a text, not just the literal meaning. The ability to read closely and critically is not required for every text that passes through our hands. Many are one-and-done. We read it once, grab the information we need, and move on. But others require a careful inspection, necessitating rereading, strategic thinking, and metacognitive questioning. These cognitive habits are established over time with the guidance of the teacher. Close reading, an instructional routine, frames a process for doing so, thereby building the expertise of readers.

Close reading as an instructional routine for elementary and middle school students is still in its first decade, although the practice has existed for nearly a century. Commonly taught in colleges and advanced high school courses, close reading has evolved to apprentice younger students into the habit (Frey & Fisher, 2013). For instructional purposes,

- The passage is short enough so that the students can reread and discuss the text within a class period

- The passage can be self-contained, but many are excerpts from longer texts the students are reading

- Rereading is done for authentic purposes, primarily to address text-dependent discussion questions posed by the teacher

- Because meaning is constructed over an extended period of time, often 30 minutes or so, students are encouraged to annotate the text in order to chronicle insights and observations

> Ten thousand hours of practice isn't the only thing that contributes to expertise; capacity is built through tasks that require critical thinking skills.

The pacing of text-dependent questions is an important scaffold for deepening knowledge (Fisher, Frey, Anderson, & Thayre, 2015b). These questions are asked in four phases:

1. The first questions are at the *literal level* and focus on the general meaning and key details of the piece. The purpose at this phase is to establish foundational knowledge to assist students in determining what the text says.

2. Phase two turns the readers' attention to the *structural elements* of the text. These structural elements include literary devices in narrative, such as foreshadowing and allusions, and expository structures, such as compare and contrast or cause and effect. The organizational features of a text might require discussion, such as the use of headings or stanzas in a poem. Word choice and vocabulary are crucial elements of the structure of the text, especially within the context of the discussion about the author's purpose for the text.

3. The third phase marks the time when students are fully applying critical thinking skills to determine *what the text means*. Text-dependent questions are designed to challenge students to form opinions with evidence, or in the case of secondary students, to engage in formal reasoning and argumentation. Questions

may also encourage students to make connections to other texts, including those that corroborate or dispute the author's position.

4. These advanced discussions lead into the final phase, which is task related: *What does the text inspire you to do?* Tasks at this phase can include written responses, investigations, a debate, or a Socratic seminar.

Figure 4.4 contains a table summarizing these phases and related question types.

Kathryn DeSoto's eleventh-grade American Literature class has been reading the play *Death of a Salesman* (Miller, 1949), and she selected the scene in Act II when Willy Loman is fired, signaling his final descent. After posing questions about the literal level of meaning to ensure that her students understand the gist, she shifts their attention to the structural level.

"Let's take a look at Willy's monologue on pages 80 and 81. Please take a moment to reread that, and think about this question: Why does Miller devote this much time to Willy's speech, when so much of the dialogue in the play has been short and clipped?"

After a few minutes, Ms. DeSoto repeats the question, inviting students to talk at their tables first. She then brings them back together as a class, saying, *"What are your thoughts about this?"*

"Well, I didn't really see this at first, but Emilio was saying that he felt like this was Willy's last big stand," Hannah offers. *"Like he's desperate, and he knows this is his last shot at making a case to keep his job."*

Emilio picks up the thread of the conversation, adding, *"And it's got the title right in there—'the death of a salesman.' Willy's talking about his dream of dying a noble death. He wants to go out of this life on top."*

As the discussion about structure winds down, Ms. DeSoto moves to the third phase, asking about what the text means. *"We've talked since the*

PHASES OF TEXT-DEPENDENT QUESTIONS

Purpose of Question	Question Focus	Question Type
Phase 1: What does the text say?	Key details	*Literal*
	General understanding	
Phase 2: How does the text work?	Author's craft and purpose	*Structural*
	Vocabulary and text structure	
Phase 3: What does the text mean?	Opinions/arguments, intertextual connections	*Inferential*
	Inferences	
Phase 4: What does the text inspire you to do?	Written responses, presentations, investigations, debates, Socratic seminar	*Interpretive*

Figure 4.4

beginning of the unit that this is considered an American tragedy. I'm curious to hear your thoughts about how this scene is a comment on the American dream. Again, I'll let you talk about this in your groups first."

After small group discussion, Dan begins, *"I was thinking about the technology in this scene. His boss wants to show off his new wire recorder. Like, we wouldn't think anything about this now, but in 1949 it was a big deal."* He continues, *"So I think Miller put that in there as a way to show that Willy is old-fashioned and behind the times."*

Ms. DeSoto asks, *"Can anyone build on Dan's idea?"*

Marta raises her hand, adding, *"And Willy's arguing the opposite. He keeps talking about Dave Singleton, who died at 84 as the greatest salesman ever. Willy's saying that some things don't change and go out of style, like being a great salesman. Except we know Willy's not."*

Ms. DeSoto nods, *"And how do we know? What's the evidence that he's not being truthful with himself?"* Several students now respond. *"He says* *on page 82 that he averaged $170 a week in 1928, but his boss says Willy never did."*

Now she is ready for the fourth phase of questioning. *"I'm going to turn this back to your groups for some investigation and writing. During the remainder of this period, locate at least two quotes on the American Dream for us to discuss tomorrow, and tell us why they are meaningful in this context. Make sure you've cited the quotes correctly. I'll collect these at the end of class so I can synthesize them for our discussion. Please read through page 97 tonight, when Willy, Bernard, and Charley meet up one final time."*

Project-Based Learning

A popular criticism of curricula is that it is "a mile wide and an inch deep." In other words, students are rarely provided time to linger on a topic and explore deeper knowledge. Instead, surface level knowledge, especially factual knowledge, is the norm. But thoughtful educators have used project- and problem-based learning (PBL) for decades to provide their students with time to investigate and grapple with challenges. These longer projects are meant to foster transfer, which occurs when learners get to apply knowledge in new and novel ways. Of course, that requires that students have developed surface and deep knowledge in advance of being presented with the problem or project.

The nature of project-based learning also requires students to exercise collaboration skills. Sixty-two percent of students report that they enjoy working on projects with other students. When we talk to students about this finding, we hear things like the following:

"When we get to work in groups, we can all share the things we have learned so far. I might have missed something that another student didn't, and vice versa. When we put our heads together, we learn the most."

"I really like working on projects with other students, as long as the teacher makes sure that everyone does their fair share of work."

Occasionally we will hear, *"I hate working with other people. I would much rather do everything on my own."*

62% of students report that they enjoy working on projects with other students.

Whether students enjoy or disdain working with others, it is important that all students develop collaboration skills. Project-based learning provides a perfect opportunity to do so.

Project-based learning describes an extended inquiry process and is an umbrella term used to describe a multitude of instructional models, including design-based learning and Genius Hour, described earlier in the chapter. Another subset is PBL, in which students are provided with an ill-defined but authentic local problem to address (How could we improve school attendance? What steps could our community take to reduce the tick population?). Each of these approaches has specific processes, but all are done in a spirit of inquiry and draw on more than one discipline.

PBL builds expertise precisely because it requires students to use knowledge in unique ways. These projects and problems can be addressed in a multitude of ways, such that no two projects or solutions are identical. In fact, the appeal of inquiry-based approaches is that the investigation is just as important as the outcomes or deliverables. These projects offer further opportunities for students to set goals, monitor their progress, reflect on their learning, and apply strategic thinking to arrive at solutions. Some PBL projects are driven by a broad essential question that doesn't seek a solution but is meant to open the door for investigation. The school where three of us work uses four schoolwide essential questions, all nominated and voted on by students, which serve as something of a "big tent" for teachers to link their projects to. As one example, the English department used the essential question *"What's worth fighting for?"* as an invitation for learning. Students were required to identify and learn about a worthy cause and build a Facebook page, with assessment based in part on the number of "likes" received from the general public. A low number of likes signaled that the page needed improvement.

Students in the primary grades are still learning how to conduct investigations, and as such their inquiry learning is led by the teacher, who organizes the project. As part of a science unit on insects, second-grade teacher Kevin Nowakowski starts his PBL with discussion about common misconceptions people have about insects. The teacher records their ideas on chart paper:

- People think all insects are bad

- People think you have to kill insects

- People don't understand that farmers need certain insects

- People are afraid of them because they look weird

"It looks to me like you're finding a problem we need to solve. How can we help our school community understand why insects are important?" he asks. As the discussion evolves, the students, under the guidance of their teacher, decide that a public relations campaign for insects is needed and that the class can help by creating informative posters about specific insects. By the next day, Mr. Nowakowski and the class have sketched a poster template that includes the name and an illustration of the insect, a box feature containing three to five fun facts about the insect, and at least one suggestion for what people can do to support the insect. Having studied insects in their science class already, his students are able to propose a variety of insect candidates, including pollinators and decomposers. The class makes a decision to include earthworms and spiders, even though they are not insects. *"That means we hafta add that to the poster,"* says Seth. *"That needs to be part of the facts."*

For the next week, students work in pairs to locate information about their assigned insect, spider, or worm. Mr. Nowakowski has curated digital resources for his students to use on the school's learning management system, and he assembled print resources for them to consult. During each class period, he meets with the 12 teams to help them gauge their progress and make decisions about next steps.

"This is a busy time, and I have to give them lots of guidance and support, but it's worth it," remarked Mr. Nowakowski. "The payoff comes when they see all the projects together." The digital posters created by the students are displayed in rotation in the cafeteria and the front office flat screen monitors so that students, teachers, and visitors can learn more about helpful insects, worms, and spiders in the region. Based on the final project, the class then critiques their collective successes and points for improvement. "One of the items they came up with is that they want to use social media with the next project!" he said.

Conclusion

A high-functioning learning community understands that failure is productive when leveraged correctly.

Challenge is necessary for learning, in terms of engagement as well as for advancement and deepening of knowledge. At their best, challenging tasks situate within the zone of proximal development, so that learners stretch their thinking. At times this may result in failure. However, a high-functioning learning community understands that failure is productive when leveraged correctly. There is a social and emotional aspect to confronting failure and pivoting to persistence, a condition that can contribute to the development of a growth mindset. But difficulty and complexity must be balanced so that students experience a range of experiences that foster fluency, stamina, strategic thinking, and expertise. No one instructional approach can magically develop all of these simultaneously. However, a comprehensive curriculum features each of these in tandem. Without attention to strategic thinking and expertise, learning stagnates. Without attention to fluency and stamina, learners get depleted too soon and become less engaged. Setting out the challenge and equipping them with the fluency, stamina, and strategic thinking tools they'll need leads to a growing expertise. And isn't that, at the end of the day, what we want for all of our students?

ENGAGEMENT

Jeremy, a freshman in high school, was a quiet student, withdrawn, and completely checked out. He showed up for class every day and didn't cause any problems, but he was clearly just putting in his time until he was old enough to drop out. He was failing nearly every class and didn't seem to care. Jeremy had effectively shut down all efforts by his teachers to get to know him and engage him in the classroom experience. His teachers had met countless times to discuss his case and had exhausted their bag of collective strategies to support struggling students. They had tried to contact his parents numerous times, with no response. They had offered to spend time with him before or after school to help him catch up, suggested peers that he might be able to study with, tried to connect with him individually during class time, and tried a host of other efforts, all of which had resulted in nothing. Bottom line: Jeremy was in the state of learning hibernation. At the end of one such meeting, Adam Sanders (school counselor) threw out a new idea. "What if next week we all focus on trying to identify even one thing *Jeremy* is interested in that we might be able use as leverage to somehow reengage him?" The team agreed.

When the team regrouped, Sandra Keen announced with a sly smile that she had something to report. She had discovered that Jeremy was interested in the outdoors. She had uncovered this in a stroke of luck when Jeremy jumped in on a class discussion about the environment. Not only had Ms. Keen been surprised when he spoke up, but also she sadly realized that she didn't even recognize his voice. *"It is really frustrating to me that no one seems care about the environment. There is nothing better than being outside, but most people I know seem to be so consumed with things like video games, and they don't give a sh*# about anything you don't need to plug in to charge!"*

Ms. Keen had to think fast. She didn't want to squelch his first real effort to engage in class discussion, but she also had to redirect the inappropriate language. *"I am impressed with your passion, Jeremy. Of course, in the classroom that passion needs to be expressed with more academic language . . . but tell us more about what you would like to see happen regarding care for the environment."*

Jeremy paused, and Ms. Keen was tempted to quickly move on, but she allowed for a bit of awkward silence before Jeremy added, *"Well, look at all the meaningless things we have clubs for at this school, like chess, debate, and even student council, and all the effort they put into planning stupid school dances, but no one cares enough to have a club about the outdoors."*

Ms. Keen responded, *"Keep in mind that those clubs all represent things that other students care about, and we should respect that. But you do make an interesting observation that there isn't any type of organized effort to support the environment and allow students opportunities to connect with the outdoors. Let's talk more about that later."* A flash of slight panic crossed Jeremy's face as he realized that he had divulged something about himself and that Ms. Keen wanted to talk to him later.

"Later" came right at the end of class, when Ms. Keen somewhat cornered him on his way out. *"Jeremy, I really appreciated your contribution in class today. What types of things do you enjoy doing in the outdoors?"* Jeremy just wanted to get out the door, so he quickly responded, *"Hiking, camping, fishing, that sort of thing."*

Ms. Keen responded, *"That's great. I really love the outdoors as well, and believe it or not I have been fly fishing since I was a kid."* Jeremy didn't respond, and it was clear he was done with the conversation. *"What would you think about us working together to start an Outdoors Club at this school? I would even be willing to connect some of your missing assignments to this if you are willing to put in the time and effort."* Again, silence. *"Just think about it, and I'll touch base with you tomorrow."*

Ms. Keen was quite doubtful that Jeremy would say yes to starting an Outdoors Club, but at least she had discovered something he was interested in, and this gave the team something to work with. They eagerly jumped into brainstorming how they could use Jeremy's interest in the outdoors and, by intentional design, reengage him in learning and school in general. It is important to note that these teachers did not view Jeremy as a problem; rather, they were focused on his potential!

The Engagement Gap

A common mantra proclaimed loud and clear by policy makers, researchers, and educators is "We must close the achievement gap." This reflects the national and international focus on standardized test scores,

When it comes to tackling the achievement gap, there must first be an understanding that this is a symptom of a much greater challenge . . . an engagement gap.

heightened each time a new set of PISA (Program for International Assessment), TIMSS (Trends in International Mathematics and Science Study), state, or localized assessment results are publicly released. Teachers, leaders, and parents frantically scan the results to see how their school stacks up and then brace themselves for whatever fallout will ensue. To be clear, we are certainly in favor of accountability. As King (2017) noted, "Without accountability, standards are meaningless and equity is a charade" (p. 28). We do, however, take issue with the narrow lens through which schools are currently viewed, and we believe that balance must be restored. We must move from a system that is driven by testing and accountability to one of trust and responsibility.

43% of students report that school is boring, and only 54% say they enjoy participating in their classes.

When it comes to tackling the achievement gap, there must first be an understanding that this is a symptom of a much greater challenge: an engagement gap. In numerous studies (Newmann, Wehlage, & Lamborn, 1992; Finn & Rock, 1997; Fredricks, Blumenfeld, & Paris, 2004; National Research Council & Institute of Medicine, 2004; Appleton, Christenson, & Furlong, 2008; Lewis, Huebner, Malone, & Valois, 2011), student engagement has been found to be predictive of a wide variety of desired academic and life outcomes, such as

- Increased academic achievement (higher grades and standardized test scores)
- Reduced drop-out rates
- Increased participation in and graduation from post-secondary programs
- Decrease in risky behaviors such as delinquency and substance abuse
- Increased satisfaction with life and overall well-being as individuals

Despite this compelling base of research leading to the importance of student engagement, motivation to engage and achieve is nearly nonexistent without frequent opportunities for students to connect with their learning in meaningful ways. Noting this, we are highly concerned that 43% of students report that school is boring, and only 54% say they enjoy participating in their classes. What is even more shocking than these data is that *no one* is surprised by them or, for that matter, feels an urgency to do something about it. It is almost like these are the accepted conditions under which we are to educate today's youth. The purpose of school is to be a place where students can learn and grow, yet only 57% of students report that school inspires them to learn. A review of the body of literature on engagement concluded that 40%–60% of high school students are "chronically disengaged" at school (Klem & Connell, 2004). If we are serious about addressing the achievement gap, we must tend to the crisis of low engagement that currently exists in far too many schools and classrooms. Every student deserves a learning experience that has high levels of *engagement by design*.

> The purpose of school is to be a place where students can learn and grow, yet only 57% of students report that school inspires them to learn.

Engagement: Overused and Misunderstood

As a group of authors, we are all fortunate to spend significant time in schools and classrooms on a regular basis, and nearly every school we interact with has a common focus on increasing student engagement. What is not common is the way engagement is defined and the strategies employed to address the crisis of disengagement. The term *engagement* is often overused and misunderstood. A principal walks into a classroom and with a quick scan observes that all students have a pencil in hand and are quietly looking at a paper in front of them. All students are engaged. Or are they?

We are electing to focus on "student engagement" as defined by Appleton et al. (2008), which is based upon the student experience in various subcontexts of life at school. Determining this level of engagement through the lens of the student experience requires a much more in-depth approach than a quick peek into a classroom. Fredricks et al. (2004)

Behavioral Engagement	• Participates in school functions
	• Attends and participates in class activities and discussions
	• Follows school rules
	• Studies
	• Completes assignments
Cognitive Engagement	• Desires challenge
	• Self-regulates
	• Plans, monitors, and evaluates one's thinking and learning
Emotional Engagement	• Comfortable talking to peers
	• Engages in group learning
	• Asks questions of teachers
	• Interested, inquisitive, and curious about academic content

Figure 5.1

breaks student engagement down into three interrelated dimensions: behavioral, cognitive, and emotional (see Figure 5.1). Behavioral and cognitive engagement were introduced in Chapter 1 and will be further discussed in the following sections, along with emotional engagement. "Engagement by design" means that teachers must intentionally tend to the behavioral, cognitive, and emotional engagement of students in the learning experience.

Behavioral Engagement

Behavioral engagement reflects academic behaviors and actions such as participating in school functions, attending and contributing to class activities and discussions, following school rules, studying, and completing assignments.

As a part of the requirements for Cynthia Jenkins's social studies class, students are invited to earn Citizen Action Points (CAPs) for putting their learning about civic responsibility into action. Students can earn CAPs for participating in school events, volunteering, engaging in peer tutoring, and most important, coming up with their own ideas to demonstrate meaningful engagement in the school and community beyond.

Cognitive Engagement

Cognitive engagement refers to the psychological effort students put into learning and mastering content. This is observed when students desire challenge, self-regulate their learning, and enact metacognitive strategies such as planning, monitoring, and evaluating their thinking and learning experience.

At the beginning of each school year, Brenda Thompson teaches a quick lesson to her students on Bloom's Taxonomy (Bloom, 1956). In groups, students are asked to create a graphic representation of the various levels of learning. Ms. Thompson is continually amazed at the creative twist students place on the concept when creating their graphics. This lesson serves as an anchor point for students in analyzing their own level of engagement in Ms. Thompson's class. *"Today I need you to prepare your brains to work hard, as we will be analyzing and evaluating some new material."* Students sit up straight and are reminded that *they* have control over the amount of effort they put into their learning.

Emotional Engagement

Emotional engagement involves how students feel about their relationships in the school environment, primarily with teachers and peers, and their general sense of belonging in the school community. Students who are emotionally engaged are comfortable talking to other students, engage in group learning, and ask questions of teachers. Emotional engagement also extends to the relationship students have with academic content and is observed when students are interested, inquisitive, and curious about the topic being studied.

HEART AT PEACE VERSUS HEART AT WAR

Heart at Peace	Heart at War
Others are PEOPLE:	Others are OBJECTS:
• Hopes, needs, cares, and fears of peers are as real to me as my own	• Peers are obstacles, vehicles, and irrelevant to me
• More likely to engage respectfully with one another	• Easy to judge and engage in unkind behaviors

Figure 5.2

Priority number one for Andrew Delgado is creating a positive classroom environment where every student feels part of the class community and also valued as a unique individual. He holds his students to the highest of standards when it comes to respecting one another, and he continually models respect in the way he engages with students and colleagues. Mr. Delgado shares with students an excerpt from *The Anatomy of Peace* (Arbinger Institute, 2006), which presents students with the opportunity either to view their peers as objects and operate with a heart at war against others or to see peers as humans and act with a heart at peace when engaging with them (see Figure 5.2). When we view others as objects, it is easy to judge and engage in unkind behaviors. But when we see others as humans and get to know them, we are more likely to engage respectfully with one another.

Mr. Delgado's starting point for building this classroom culture is having students introduce themselves and complete the sentence *"You might be surprised to know about me . . ."* Yes, it takes a full class period to complete the exercise, but Mr. Delgado strongly believes the investment of time is well worth the foundation that is set for a classroom culture in which all students and their voices are of the highest value. Mr. Delgado (like all of the incredible teachers highlighted throughout this book) is a true master at engagement by design. This approach to student engagement—tending to the cognitive, behavioral, and emotional

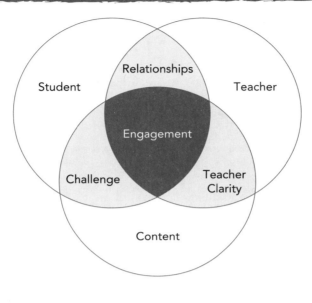

Figure 5.3

experience of students—leads to a rich understanding for teachers and students of what it truly means to be engaged (Wang, Willet, & Eccles, 2011; Christenson, Reschly, & Wylie, 2012; Appleton et al., 2008).

Bringing It All Together

In Figure 5.3, we return to the Balanced Model for Optimal Learning originally presented in Chapter 1, which highlights the **student**, the **teacher**, and the **content**. These factors must operate in harmony with one another; they have significant impact on academic and personal outcomes.

There are *four intersections* that lead to the heart of this model, which comes to life when the teacher, student, and content are meaningfully connected. Chapter 2 focused on the intersection between student

SUMMATIVE EQUATION FOR STUDENT ENGAGEMENT*

$$Engagement = STC + \sum_{SW+P}^{R+TC+CH} V$$

* Thank you to Judith A. Deeley, mathematics teacher, Guardian Angels School, for helping us develop our concept of student engagement as a mathematical formula.

Figure 5.4

and teacher, where relationships are formed. Chapter 3 addressed the concept of teacher clarity, which is critical within the intersection of teacher and content. And the importance of challenge, the intersection between student and content, was discussed in Chapter 4. The aim of this final chapter is to focus on the middle intersection: **Engagement**.

The Engagement Equation

As we bring these pieces together and move toward the ideal engagement by design for students and teachers, consider the student engagement equation in Figure 5.4.

Look complex? The more complex the problem, the more satisfying the solution! Let's break it down, for every component of the equation is of great importance. The first component, STC, represents the three factors already discussed:

- **Students (S)** enter the classroom to gather, discover, process, understand, integrate, and ultimately learn information.
- **Teachers (T)** enter the classroom to share, present, guide, instruct, scaffold, and facilitate students in gaining knowledge. They must know content and possess the skills necessary to present information in a format that is understandable and relevant.
- **Content (C)** represents information to be learned and how that information is discovered and shared by both the student and the teacher.

The top variables in the equation, R + TC + CH, signify the other concepts covered in previous chapters:

- **Relationships (R)** that are healthy between teachers and students are built upon trust and create an environment of safety in which students can focus on learning and the teacher can learn more about the student and his or her interests.

- **Teacher Clarity (TC)** is the combination of teachers knowing what they are supposed to be teaching, informing students about what they are supposed to be learning, and reaching agreements with students about the success criteria.

- **Challenge (CH)** is the balance of difficulty and complexity that affords students a range of experiences that foster fluency, stamina, strategic thinking, and content expertise.

Now it is time to address the components that ensure *students* are at the heart of the engagement process, SW + P:

- **Self-Worth (SW)** exists when students know they are valued as individuals in the school community and when they have someone in their life who believes in them.

- **Purpose (P)** exists when students take responsibility for who and what they are becoming.

Finally, we are putting our stake in the ground and declaring Student Voice (V) as the **most** critical component in the entire equation. For without it, we cannot help students develop Self-Worth (SW) and identify Purpose (P) in their life, build trusting and lasting Relationships (R) with students, determine how to provide the appropriate level of Challenge (CH) and support, and ultimately deliver the Clarity (C) in teaching that allows us to reach all students.

- **Voice (V)** means students are able to express their thoughts and opinions, and they also take responsibility in turning their voice into action to advocate for themselves and others.

The sum of this complex equation is a level of **engagement** we dream about. At this point, you are either impressed with our cleverness or

> We are putting our stake in the ground and declaring Student Voice as the **most** critical component in the entire equation.

highly confused. If it is the latter, hang with us! Let's further explore the new components we have just introduced in the equation.

Voice (V)

Students want to be understood and should be expected to share their voice as part of the learning process. The school and classroom should be safe places where students can express their honest opinions and concerns, ask questions, and have meaningful decision-making opportunities. When students believe they have a voice in school, they are seven times more likely to be academically motivated! Yet only 43% of students report that adults in their school listen to students' suggestions, and 44% believe they have a voice in decision making at school. See Figure 5.5 for a description of the differences between students with limited voice and those who exercise their voice.

Student voice is far more than an opinion survey given once a year. Students must take responsibility not only for expressing their thoughts but also for turning their voice into action to advocate for themselves and to help others. Equally important, adults in schools must give students opportunities to be a part of solution-oriented decision making and actions to improve the school. These opportunities must be afforded to all students, particularly those identified as at-risk and in need of authentic connection to the school community. Empowering students to take their voice and turn it into meaningful action is what genuine student voice is all about.

An excellent starting place is to conduct student focus groups to gain a deeper understanding of student beliefs and perceptions about their experience at school. These groups intentionally engage a wide variety of student voices, including those that may typically be silent or viewed as challenging. It is important to then take action based on what is learned from students *and* clearly communicate with all members of the school community what actions have been taken as a result of the student feedback. If that loop is not closed, students may think their voices are not being valued, even if the school is indeed listening and taking action.

> When students believe they have a voice in school, they are seven times more likely to be academically motivated.

> Only 43% of students report that adults in their school listen to students' suggestions.

VOICE (V)

Students with limited voice . . .	Students with voice . . .
Believe no one cares what they think	Effectively express their thoughts with confidence that someone is listening
Have the attitude, "I am just a student"	Know what they say truly matters
Complain and expect someone else to deal with their concerns	Strategically share their concerns and express what they are willing to do to be part of a solution
Expect the school to take care of them	Know they are an important part of the school community and share in responsibility for the kind of place it is

Figure 5.5

See the following for more information on conducting student focus groups:

Grades K–2: http://quagliainstitute.org/dmsView/FocusGroupsK2

Grades 3–12: http://quagliainstitute.org/dmsView/FocusGroups

Remember Jeremy, the disengaged student we introduced at the beginning of the chapter? Let's catch up with him and consider the ways in which honoring his voice might engage him in learning. The next day, Ms. Keen again caught Jeremy on his way out the door, despite his best efforts to evade her. *"Did you do any thinking about the idea of starting an Outdoors Club here at school?"*

Without making eye contact, Jeremy flatly responded, *"I don't think so."*

Ms. Keen was desperate. *"What if we could organize a backpacking trip for club members?"*

Jeremy looked her in the eye. Now he seemed at least a little interested. *"Are you serious?"*

"Yes, but I am also serious about getting you caught up in class," Ms. Keen responded.

"Would all of my missing work be excused if I do this club thing?"

Ms. Keen smiled, *"Nice try. Not excused, but I am willing to work together to link what we've been studying and assignments to your Outdoor Club efforts. But you have to meet me half way."*

Jeremy stuck out his hand. *"You have a deal."*

Self-Worth (SW)

> Self-worth occurs when students know they are uniquely valued members of the school community; have a person in their lives they can trust and learn from; and believe they have the ability to achieve—academically, personally, and socially. (Quaglia & Corso, 2014, pp. 23–24)

For students to experience maximum engagement in the learning process, they must feel like they belong in the school community while also being recognized, appreciated, and celebrated for their uniqueness as individuals. Belonging to any group, including a school community, should not come at the expense of sacrificing one's individuality. Rather, when the unique personalities, skills, and talents of individuals are embraced, belonging to the larger community becomes truly meaningful. Sadly, only 40% of students believe they are a valued member of their school community, a problem that must be addressed. If students do not feel like they are a valued, we cannot expect them to feel safe, be motivated to engage in the learning experience, or master required academic content and necessary life skills to be successful beyond school.

Only 40% of students believe they are a valued member of their school community.

Self-worth is also cultivated in students when they are recognized for their growth and accomplishments. It is good to celebrate academic achievement measured by grades and tests;

SELF-WORTH (SW)

Student lacking self-worth . . .	Students with self-worth . . .
Think they don't matter	Know they are recognized and celebrated for who they are
Perceive the most important thing in school is grades	Believe effort, perseverance, and being a good citizen are important
Believe no one cares about them	Can identify at least one adult in school with whom they can share both successes and challenges
Are afraid to fail or to succeed	Learn from their mistakes and are proud of their successes

Figure 5.6

however, students should know that progress is valued over perfection. Additionally, academic growth should only represent a fraction of the student accomplishments being celebrated in schools. Things such as effort, perseverance, and citizenship should be recognized and celebrated equally with academic outcomes.

Students experience self-worth when someone in their life believes in them; something they only know when we tell them and show them on a consistent basis (see Figure 5.6). Teachers cannot assume that students know we care for them and believe in them. In fact, 88% of students carry a self-belief that they can be successful, but a significantly lower 73% report that their teachers believe in them and expect them to be successful. *This must change.* Students need teachers to be intentional in setting high expectations, letting them know we believe they can be successful and that we will support them on their journey to reaching their aspirations. When students have a sense of self-worth, they are six times more likely to be academically motivated to learn.

Video 13
Fostering Self-Worth

*resources.corwin.com/
engagementbydesign*

When students have a sense of self-worth, they are six times more likely to be academically motivated to learn.

Although there is always room for improvement, we do observe examples of effective practices that support the development of strong student self-worth. The importance of learning and using student names as a regular practice was discussed in a previous chapter, but it is so important we believe it to be worth repeating. Knowing names, however, is just a starting point. Follow that with learning about something individual students are interested in: a strength, a fear, and, most important, their hopes and dreams for the future.

Another powerful strategy to support the development of self-worth is to intentionally teach students skills related to perseverance, resiliency, and the power of supporting one another in the journey of learning and life. Students must be provided with an environment in which they are encouraged to take healthy risks—a place where it is safe to both fail and succeed. Currently, 62% of students report that their teachers help them learn from mistakes, 33% of students are afraid to try something new if they think they may fail, and only 39% say that students are supportive of one another.

Interestingly, the fear of judgment if one is successful also exists, with only 55% of students reporting they are excited to tell their friends when they get good grades. When digging deeper in student focus groups, we frequently hear students share stories of being judged and even ridiculed if they move from whatever category of achievement they have traditionally experienced. If a C student suddenly starts pulling A's, she may pose a threat to the traditional A students and, at the same time, be outcast by her previous counterparts in the land of C grades. As so many students have told us, "It is just safer to stay where you belong."

Alexandria Amador is a master at creating an environment that capitalizes on the concept of collaborative competition. Although all students are striving to do their individual best, they also know they have a responsibility in her class to support their peers. Her constant mantra is, *"When I get better, we all get better, and when we all get better, I get better."* She has created a series of safety nets that allow students to celebrate and learn from their failures as an important part of the learning process. Students are encouraged to share both their failures and successes with their classmates as a regular practice in her classroom, and she does the same, modeling by sharing her own successes and epic failures and how those moments have been leveraged into progress.

Finally, consider conducting a celebration systems audit in which you analyze the current ways your school recognizes students. If a majority, or all, of the celebration focuses on the highest academic performers, consider developing strategies for recognizing things like creativity, innovation, growth, and kindness. Engage students in the process of determining how to best celebrate in your school, as well as identifying a wide variety of areas and skills deemed worthy of recognition.

Although Jeremy didn't really care about anything he was learning in his classes, he decided that he would do what was necessary to start an Outdoors Club. He had a number of friends who were interested, especially in the idea of a backpacking trip and the opportunity to sleep under the stars. And although he would never admit it to anyone, it did mean something to him that Ms. Keen was going out on a limb for him. He had never talked to a teacher as much as he had talked to Ms. Keen in the last few weeks, and he was beginning to believe that she actually liked him and believed in him.

One of the first things Jeremy discovered when they starting working through the process of gaining administrative approval to start an Outdoors Club was that students must be passing all classes in order to participate in extracurricular activities, including school clubs. This meant that he needed to get caught up not only in Ms. Keen's class but also in all of his classes, which seemed like a daunting and impossible task. He went to Ms. Keen and told her he was out. After much persistence and an impressive display of persuasion, Ms. Keen convinced Jeremy to at least give it a try. She assured him that the other teachers were on board

> **33% of students are afraid to try something new if they think they may fail, and only 39% say that students are supportive of one another.**

> **Students fear judgment if they succeed; only 55% report that they are excited to tell their friends when they get good grades.**

for helping him get caught up and that she was personally there to support him. The school's philosophy that it's never too late to learn drove these teachers never to give up on students. Ms. Keen was on a mission and told Jeremy she was willing to do whatever it would take, and deep inside, Jeremy wanted to believe her.

Purpose (P)

> Purpose exists when students take responsibility for who and what they are becoming. This involves not only choosing a career but also deciding to be involved, responsible members of their community. (Quaglia & Corso, 2014, p. 24)

Schools have an incredible opportunity and *responsibility* to help students determine *what* they want to be when they grow up and, equally important, *who* they want to be. Teachers can support this effort by challenging students to think about the characteristics that accompany successful and rewarding work. William Damon (2009), who literally wrote *the* book on purpose (*The Path to Purpose: How Young People Find Their Calling in Lif*e) defines it as "a stable generalized intention to accomplish something that is at the same time meaningful to the self and consequential for the world beyond self" (p. 33). Developing a true sense of purpose involves becoming the leader in one's own life, taking on responsibility for self and others, and having the confidence to take action and make a difference in the world. One of the most profound findings in our own studies has shown that when students find purpose in their experience at school, they are 17 times more likely to be academically motivated to learn.

When students find purpose in their experience at school, they are 17 times more likely to be academically motivated to learn.

Noting the significant impact purpose has on student motivation to learn, we are gravely concerned that only 38% of students believe their classes help them to understand what is happening in their everyday lives. And sadly, when we look at these data by grade level, the longer students are in school, the less connection they see between what they are learning and their lives outside of school. There is a tremendous need to better connect the experience at school to the current lives of students and who they want to become in the future.

Leadership is not an experience that should be reserved only for those on student council or granted a title like "captain" or "team leader." Leadership must be redefined as something that *all* students will experience through meaningful opportunities to lead, make decisions, and take on responsibility for themselves and others. Leadership skills should be explicitly taught in schools and then exercised in connection with student interests and passions.

Another strategy for developing purpose is to encourage students to move from admiring their problems to living with a solution-oriented mindset. Like all humans, students need to have their struggles recognized and validated. However, we must provide them with strategies and supports to move beyond their challenges and take steps in the present to achieve their goals and aspirations for the future. This leads into supporting students in becoming effective decision makers, an ability that requires skills in analyzing situations, weighing pros and cons, considering possible consequences, and applying lessons learned from previous experiences. We have talked at length about celebrating successes and learning to replicate positive results, but it is also important to learn from failures by accepting consequences, adjusting, and moving forward when desired results are not met. See Figure 5.7 for a description of the differences between students with purpose and those who lack it.

Returning to Jeremy's story, we will explore the role of purpose in facilitating engagement. A significant amount of administrative discussion and negotiation led to the official establishment of the Capital High School Outdoors Club, with Jeremy provisionally listed as the Organizing Student Sponsor. If he didn't pull his grades up by the end of the semester, the deal was off.

Jeremy adamantly did not want to be called the president of the Outdoors Club, as he had very strong opinions about students with

> Schools have an incredible opportunity and *responsibility* to help students determine *what* they want to be when they grow up and, equally important, *who* they want to be.

Students lacking purpose . . .	Students with purpose . . .
Think they must have a title to be a leader	Believe everyone is a leader
Believe teachers are responsible for their success or failure	Take responsibility for who they are and will become
Are apathetic and go with the flow	Stand up for causes they believe in
Believe their future is already determined for them	Spend more time thinking about where they are going and less time worrying about where they are from

Figure 5.7

official club titles (don't forget his original outburst declaring all clubs at the school "stupid"). But for all intents and purposes, Jeremy did step into a leadership role. He had found purpose in creating a club that had significant meaning not only to him but also to dozens of other students who were finding a connection to the school community, many for the first time.

Every Wednesday at lunch, Room 217 became the place to explore all things outdoors, including remedies for foot fungus from hiking in wet socks, the most beautiful places on the planet to adventure, and how the club might contribute to local conservation efforts. Ms. Keen worked with Jeremy to translate the content from missing assignments into actions he could apply in the Outdoors Club. She provided substantial support during the first few meetings, and over time she gradually released more and more responsibility to Jeremy, a task that often required her amazing skills in persuasion.

Only 38% of students believe their classes help them to understand what is happening in their everyday lives.

One day, a club member caught Jeremy in the hall and asked him whether their lunch meeting was going to be cancelled because Ms. Keen was attending a professional learning event. Without even thinking, Jeremy said to spread the word that they would still be meeting. He knew the plan and realized he was comfortable enough to run the meeting even without Ms. Keen. The meeting went well, and Jeremy had club members write notes on the board to Ms. Keen letting her know they had missed her. Jeremy had discovered his purpose. He became a leader in the eyes of others and in his own as well.

Engagement

Now that we have fully explored the components of the Summative Equation for Student Engagement, it is time to discuss the result. Why should we work so hard to understand and apply such a complex equation? What should expected outcomes look like? Most important, how will this benefit students?

The type of engagement by design that we dream about can only exist when a classroom culture is underpinned by trust and respect among and between teachers and students. With this foundation established, students are invited, expected, and safe to actively participate in the learning experience. When students are engaged and connect learning with their everyday lives, they are 14 times more likely to be academically motivated. To create this type of engaging learning environment, teachers must become masters of relevance! Ask students about their interests in and out of school, and work with students to create connections between their interests and the learning experience. Seek to connect content to personal identity, other classes, everyday life, current events, and the future.

We also challenge you to embrace fun and excitement in learning. We believe that learning can be, and should be, fun for both students and teachers. This does not mean that students are laughing their way through every minute of learning while playing games (though we do love games!), but the enthusiasm expressed by a truly passionate teacher, even in the most difficult of learning moments, is highly contagious and naturally draws students into learning. Authentic fun and excitement is about being so engaged that one loses track of time and space. Csikszentmihalyi (1990) describes this phenomenon as an individual

Leadership must be redefined as something that *all* students will experience through meaningful opportunities to lead, make decisions, and take on responsibility for themselves and others.

being so fully immersed in something she achieves an optimal state of intrinsic motivation known as "flow." We hear about athletes "being in the zone." Our model of engagement is at its optimal point when students are in a learning zone.

Think about something you enjoy doing so much that hours can whiz by before you know it. Russ and Lisa are both avid fishers and can easily spend an entire day fully engaged in the pursuit of the perfect catch, with no worry or thought about the world beyond the middle of the river. Similarly, we are guessing that when Jeremy is on a hike in the mountains, he is not looking at his watch waiting for the experience to end. Instead, he is in the moment, and time seems to fly by. The challenge for teachers is to create that feeling and experience when it comes to math, science, foreign language, social studies, English, and so on.

> **When students are engaged and connect learning with their everyday lives, they are 14 times more likely to be academically motivated.**

Let students know that you will give maximum effort to creating engaging lessons and that you expect maximum effort in return as they engage in learning. Engagement by design is not the sole responsibility of the teacher. Teach students strategies that provide opportunities for continual self-reflection regarding their level of engagement, as well as actions to persevere and reengage when they are tempted to check out. For example, we utilize a strategy called Check Up From the Neck Up, which asks students to answer three questions about their engagement during a lesson:

- When was I most engaged?
- When was I least engaged?
- What could I have done to be more engaged?

Video 14
Student Self-Refection on Engagement

resources.corwin.com/ engagementbydesign

This guides students in identifying their patterns of engagement and developing strategies for recognizing when they struggle and how to persevere through those times of challenge. The primary intent of this strategy is to support students in taking responsibility for their engagement in the learning process, but information gleaned from this type of self-analysis can also be incredibly helpful to teachers in recognizing high and low points of engagement during a lesson from the perspective of students. Teachers are then able to adjust future instruction to replicate practices leading to high levels of engagement and minimize moments when students are tempted to check out.

Engaged Students

We have tapped into the voices of countless teachers and students to see how they would define ideal engagement. We all want it, but what does it *look like, sound like, feel like*? Interestingly, students and teachers alike begin with describing what engagement is *not*. When asked to describe themselves when they *are* engaged in learning, students often begin with statements like, "I don't look at the clock even once," and "I don't want to poke my eyes out with a pencil," and "I am not thinking about all of the other things I would rather be doing." Non-examples are indeed important to identify, but we need to start focusing on what engagement *is* so we can model it, experience it, and identify desired results. What are the consistent behaviors identified in engaged students? What are the characteristics of engaging classrooms? And what are the expected outcomes of highly engaging learning experiences?

Students struggle to move beyond the non-examples into describing what engagement *does* looks like. Thus, the task at hand: *teaching students what ideal engagement looks like and how to identify it in their own learning.* What are the consistent behaviors identified in engaged students?

- **Engaged students lose track of time and space.** As previously mentioned, students who are meaningfully engaged lose track of time and space and become so immersed in the learning experience they will say, "I can't believe class is already over! Where did the time go?" The same is true for teachers. If we are being honest, there are days when teachers are watching the clock tick by at a snail's pace and other days when time flies by. Just know that if time is dragging for you as the

Video 15
What Does Engagement
Look Like and Feel Like?

resources.corwin.com/
engagementbydesign

teacher, it is likely passing at a painful pace for your students as well. Conversely, if the hands on the clock are a non-factor for teacher and student, you are well on your way to the zone of ideal engagement.

- **Engaged students are not afraid to fail or succeed**, and they gain as much satisfaction from effort and perseverance as they do from a letter grade. They truly believe it is acceptable to fail and that much can be learned from experiences that did not initially lead to desired results. Like the Little Engine That Could, these students will try, try again. On the flip side, engaged students are also comfortable being successful, and they are willing to share their successes with others. They are willing to learn from the experiences of others and allow peers to benefit from their own successes and failures.

> Only 58% of students report feeling comfortable asking questions in class.

- **Engaged students are able to express their honest opinions and concerns** in the classroom and beyond. Unfortunately, only 58% of students report feeling comfortable asking questions in class.

- In outlining a vision for the ideal school that *does* value student voice and provide opportunities for students to learn from successes and failures, the authors of *Aspire High: Imagining Tomorrow's School Today* have described meaningful engagement as the following: **Engaged students are deeply involved in the learning process** as characterized by enthusiasm, a desire to learn new things, and a willingness to take positive, healthy steps toward the future.

- **Engaged students are emotionally, intellectually, and behaviorally invested in learning** (Quaglia, Corso, Fox, & Dykes, 2017, p. 53).

For this deep investment in learning to be possible, it is also critical that students have someone in their life who believes in them and they can turn to for support. A summary of the characteristics of engaged students can be found in Figure 5.8.

ENGAGED STUDENTS

Engaged Students

- Feel like they belong because they are recognized for who they are
- Have someone in their life they can turn to for support, encouragement, and praise
- Gain as much satisfaction from knowing they persevered and gave effort as from receiving a letter grade
- Continually ask "why?" and "why not?"
- Lose track of time and space when learning
- Are not afraid to fail or succeed
- Take on leadership roles and the responsibility that goes with them
- Possess the confidence to take action on causes they believe in
- Express their voice in a way that is recognized, valued, and heard

Figure 5.8

Engaged Classrooms

It can also be easier for students to describe a non-engaging classroom than to explain what an engaged classroom *does* look like. "We file in like zombies and go through the motions of pretending to learn." "We do the minimum work required to get by." "The only expectation I have is that I will be bored—and I am always right!" We would describe the highly engaged classrooms we observe as places where everyone is a teacher and a learner and all voices are heard, respected, and valued. Effective communication and meaningful conversation exist between students and teachers. Collaboration between peers is not an assigned event but a natural way of being.

One of our colleagues whose work we deeply respect, Jim Knight, is a master at the art of effective communication. He has developed the following Better Conversations Beliefs:

1. I see conversation partners as equals.

2. I want to hear what others have to say.

3. I believe people should have a lot of autonomy.

4. I don't judge others.

5. Conversations should be back and forth.

6. Conversations should be life-giving. (Knight, 2016, p. 24)

Jim's work has caused us to reflect on the ways in which we converse with students. What would happen if we applied these Better Conversations Beliefs when engaging in dialogue with students?

1. I see *students* as equal conversation partners.

2. I want to hear what *students* have to say.

3. I believe *students* should have a lot of autonomy.

4. Conversations with *students* should be back and forth.

5. Conversations with *students* should be life-giving.

The way in which we communicate with students is of critical importance, and we believe that adopting these Better Conversations Beliefs can have a profound impact on classroom dialogue. Students know when adults are authentically interested in what they have to say, and they are equally attuned to condescending or patronizing responses. The most engaging classrooms we observed are filled with constant and respectful dialogue between teachers and students.

Additionally, engaging classrooms reflect fluid lessons that are continually evolving and are not constrained by time. Students take responsibility for their own learning, and collaborating with one another is the norm. See Figure 5.9 for a list of characteristics of engaged classrooms.

Engaged Student Outcomes

We have described what engaged students and engaging classrooms look like, but we believe it is important to also explore the outcomes we

ENGAGED CLASSROOMS

Engaged Classrooms
• Learning is not constrained by time
• Lessons are fluid and continually evolving
• An atmosphere of respect and understanding exists
• Student collaboration is the norm
• Meaningful conversation flows between students and teachers
• Responsibility replaces accountability
• Everyone is a teacher and a learner
• All voices are heard and valued
• There is a harmonious relationship between skills and challenges
• Personalization (knowing the students) influences the content

Figure 5.9

should expect from engaged students and classrooms. This is where the rubber meets the road . . . the reason why it is worth working so hard to foster meaningful engagement!

- **Engaged students develop a greater sense of self-worth** and appreciation for the ideas of others, even when their perspectives differ.

- **Engaged students have a strong sense of purpose** and understanding of who they are, which enables them to think beyond themselves and consider the impact of their actions upon others.

- **Engaged students have an increased spirit of adventure and excitement for learning** that leads to a willingness to take on academic challenges. They actively explore things they are curious about and apply creativity to their learning experience.

- **Engaged students believe in themselves**. Engaged students take pride in their learning and the actions they take in the classroom and beyond. They know they can make a difference in the world, and they are able to dream about the future and also take steps in the present to achieve those dreams.

We hope you are nodding your head and thinking, "Yes! That is exactly what I want from my students!" Interestingly, we find the same outcomes to be true of teachers who are highly engaged (Quaglia & Lande, 2017). We challenge you to hold yourself to the same list of outcomes because *you* are a powerful model to your students. See Figure 5.10 for a description of engaged student outcomes.

The Ending of One Story Is the Beginning of Another

In addition to helping him start an Outdoors Club, Jeremy's teachers invited him to find creative ways to connect his interest in the outdoors to the content learned in his classes. They gave him ideas to get started, but they were clear that the responsibility would ultimately be his. As most students do, Jeremy rose to the occasion. In a social studies paper, Jeremy wrote about the economic impact of conservation efforts and the struggle to entice companies to pay more now in production costs for the sake of future benefits to the environment. A series of math problems were created based on the distance and terrain of the Appalachian hiking trail, and the connections in science were endless! Jeremy conducted a study on the impact of pesticides being used by farmers on the peregrine falcon population. He led the effort to connect the Outdoors Club with a local water plant to learn more about the city's water supply and followed up with a campaign to inform the student body of easy ways in which they could help conserve water, like turning off the faucet when brushing their teeth. True to their word, Jeremy's teachers worked with him to connect his efforts to class assignments whenever possible.

Ms. Keen also kept her promise, and the year ended with the first annual Capital High Outdoors Club hiking trip. The club had experienced

ENGAGED STUDENT OUTCOMES

Engaged Student Outcomes
• Greater sense of self-worth
• Appreciation of other people's ideas
• Greater sense of purpose, understanding of "who" they are, and thinking beyond themselves
• Acceptance of different perspectives
• Excitement for learning
• Willingness to take on academic challenges
• Awareness of their own ability and potential
• Increased confidence and pride in their ability
• Mindfulness of the importance of curiosity and creativity
• Increased spirit of adventure
• Respect for themselves and others
• Awareness of the potential impact of their actions on others

Figure 5.10

significant growth over the year, and Ms. Keen was worried about getting enough faculty sponsors for the trip. She was pleasantly surprised at the number of teachers not only willing but also *wanting* to participate. The story of Jeremy and his reengagement both in and out of the classroom had spread across the school and had become a source of inspiration to other students and to teachers as well.

There was plenty of content Jeremy needed to master that did not connect to the outdoors, but the opportunity to inject his passion into the classroom experience here and there was the key to his reengagement in the classroom . . . mostly. We would not want to inaccurately paint a picture of all sunshine and roses. After barely surviving summer school and some very painful tutoring sessions (for the student and teachers alike), Jeremy graduated and proudly placed a pin on the map outside of the front office reflecting where graduates were going to college. His GPA was not the best, but with a decent SAT score and a glowing teacher recommendation from Ms. Keen praising Jeremy's academic turn-around, Jeremy had been accepted to a local community college to study wildlife biology. Jeremy had a goal for his future. He engaged in actions and learning to work toward achieving that goal. And he had experienced teachers who embraced him for who he was as an individual and allowed him to find his place of belonging in the school community. For Jeremy, the engagement gap was closed, personally and academically. And the inspiration he provided his peers led to other new clubs and organizations, such as a World Wrestling Entertainment (WWE) Club, the Cupcake Cooking Team, and a Graffiti Magic group, to name a few!

> Dreaming about tomorrow must be in balance with taking action today. Absent that engagement, we are simply in a state of imagination.

Conclusion

Engagement by design is about creating an environment in which all students thrive. It starts in the classroom, but it is designed to spill over into life. If we expect students (and teachers) to reach their fullest potential, then genuine engagement must become the norm, a natural way of being. Engagement takes root when schools ensure staff and students are deeply involved in the learning process, demonstrate enthusiasm and desire to learn new things, and willingly take positive, healthy steps toward the future.

"Dream big" and "shoot for the stars" have become commonplace phrases, all with great intentions. But they are missing a key component for success: engagement. Dreaming about tomorrow must be in balance with taking action today. Absent that engagement, we are simply in a state of imagination.

Balance is a term sprinkled throughout this book, which aptly applies to engagement. We believe there is a delicate balance between the student, teacher, and content that, when achieved, allows children to flourish with a clear sense of purpose. When imbalanced, students' confusion and isolation leads to disengagement. As we reflect on the Summative Equation for Student Engagement, there are several educational scales to balance in our efforts to support engagement by design:

Content Demands and Student Interests

Being laser focused on what "must" be taught at the expense of what should be taught to better meet students' interests can cause incredible boredom—the antithesis of engagement.

Accountability and Responsibility

There is no denying the fact that our current educational system is driven by accountability, but we would argue that it must be balanced with responsibility. Accountability is usually commanded from an external entity. Responsibility is an internal force that fuels self-worth, drives personal challenges and sustains engagement in learning, and powers success.

Talking and Listening

Educators are the content experts and have the capacity to transmit knowledge to their students with clarity, which is critical, but the learning process is shortchanged if it is only the teacher's voice being heard. By listening to the voices of students, teachers model that learning is a two-way street and demonstrate that they value and can learn from their students' insights.

Each and every one of you possesses the ability to be a master of engagement by design. It is time to challenge yourself to balance the scales for your students. Never forget that wonderful surprises are just waiting to happen, and that all your hopes and dreams for an engaged learning environment are well within your, and your students', reach!

References

Afflerbach, P., Pearson, P. D., & Paris, S. G. (2008). Clarifying differences between reading skills and reading strategies. *The Reading Teacher, 61*(5), 364–373.

Ainsworth, L. (2011). *Rigorous curriculum design: How to create curricular units of study that align standards, instruction, and assessment.* Englewood, CO: Lead + Learn Press.

Anyon, Y., Gregory, A., Stone, S., Farrar, J., Jenson, J. M., McQueen, J., . . . Simmons, J. (2016). Restorative interventions and school discipline sanctions in a large urban school district. *American Educational Research Journal, 53*(6), 1663–1797.

Appleton, J. J., Christenson, S. L., & Furlong, M. J. (2008). Student engagement with school: Critical conceptual and methodological issues of the construct. *Psychology in the Schools, 45*, 369–386.

Arbinger Institute. (2006). *The anatomy of peace: Resolving the heart of conflict.* San Francisco, CA: Berrett-Koehler.

Berninger, V. W., & Swanson, H. L. (1994). Modifying Hayes and Flower's model of skilled writing to explain beginning and developing writing. In J. S. Carlson (Series Ed.) & E. C. Butterfield (Vol. Ed.), *Advances in cognition and educational practice: Vol. 2. Children's writing: Toward a process theory of the development of skilled writing* (pp. 57–81). Greenwich, CT: JAI Press.

Bloom, B. (1956). *Bloom's taxonomy of educational objectives, handbook I: The cognitive domain.* White Plains, NY: Longman.

Caulk, N. (1994). Comparing teacher and student responses to written work. *TESOL Quarterly, 28*(1), 181–188.

Christenson, S. L., Reschly, A. L., & Wylie, C. (2012). *The handbook of research on student engagement.* New York, NY: Springer Science.

City, E. A., Elmore, R. F., Fiarman, S. E., & Tietel, L. (2009). *Instructional rounds in education: A network approach to improving teaching and learning.* Boston, MA: Harvard University Press.

Cornelius-White, J. (2007). Learner-centered teacher-student relationships are effective: A meta-analysis. *Review of Educational Research, 77*(1), 113–143.

Csikszentmihalyi, M. (1990). *Flow: The psychology of optimal experience.* New York, NY: Harper & Row.

Damon, W. (2009). *The path to purpose: How young people find their calling in life.* New York, NY: The Free Press.

Donovan, M. S., & Bransford, J. D. (Eds.). (2005). *How students learn: History, mathematics, and science in the classroom*. Committee on How People Learn: A Targeted Report for Teachers. Division on Behavioral and Social Sciences and Education. Washington, DC: National Academies.

Duckworth, A. (2016). *Grit: The power of passion and perseverance*. New York, NY: Scribner.

Duehren, A. M., & Thompson, D. C. (2016). In debate over names, history and race relations collide. *The Harvard Crimson*. Retrieved from http://www.thecrimson .com/article/2016/1/19/faust-name-title-changes-/

Dweck, C. S. (2006). *Mindset: The new psychology of success*. New York, NY: Ballantine Books.

Ennen, N., Stark, E. E., & Lassiter, A. (2015). The importance of trust for satisfaction, motivation, and academic performance in student learning groups. *Social Psychology of Education, 18*(3), 615–633.

Falk, A. (2012). Teachers learning from professional development in elementary science: Reciprocal relations between formative assessment and pedagogical content knowledge. *Science Education, 96*(2), 265–290.

Fendick, F. (1990). *The correlation between teacher clarity of communication and student achievement gain: A meta-analysis* (Unpublished doctoral dissertation). University of Florida, Gainesville.

Finn, J. D., & Rock, D. A. (1997). Academic success among students at risk for school failure. *Journal of Applied Psychology, 82*, 221–234.

Fisher, D., & Frey, N. (2010). *Guided instruction: How to develop confident and successful learners*. Alexandria, VA: ASCD.

Fisher, D., & Frey, N. (2011). *The purposeful classroom: How to structure lessons with learning goals in mind*. Alexandria, VA: ASCD.

Fisher, D., & Frey, N. (2014). *Better learning through structured teaching: A framework for the gradual release of responsibility* (2nd ed.). Alexandria, VA: ASCD.

Fisher, D., Frey, N., Anderson, H., & Thayre, M. (2015a). *Text-dependent questions: Pathways to close and critical reading, grades 6–12*. Thousand Oaks, CA: Corwin.

Fisher, D., Frey, N., Anderson, H., & Thayre, M. (2015b). *Text-dependent questions: Pathways to close and critical reading, grades K–5*. Thousand Oaks, CA: Corwin.

Fisher, D., Frey, N., & Hattie, J. (2016). *Visible learning for literacy: Implementing the practices that work best to accelerate student learning*. Thousand Oaks, CA: Corwin.

Flanders, N. (1970). *Analyzing teacher behavior*. Reading, MA: Addison-Wesley.

Flavell, J. H. (1979). Metacognition and cognitive monitoring: A new area of cognitive-developmental inquiry. *American Psychologist, 34*, 906–911.

Frayer, D. A., Frederick, W. C., & Klausmeier, H. J. (1969). *A schema for testing the level of concept mastery (Working paper No. 16)*. Madison, WI: Wisconsin Research and Development Center for Cognitive Learning.

Fredricks, J. A., Blumenfeld, P. C., & Paris, A. H. (2004). School engagement: Potential of the concept, state of the evidence. *Review of Educational Research, 74,* 59–109.

Frey, N., & Fisher, D. (2013). *Rigorous reading: Five access points for helping students comprehend complex texts, K–12.* Thousand Oaks, CA: Corwin.

Gagne, R. M. (1967). The acquisition of knowledge. In R. J. Shumway (Ed.), *Research in mathematics education* (pp. 6–20). Reston, VA: National Council of Teachers of Mathematics.

Gallup, Inc., & NWEA. (2016). *Make assessment work for all students: Multiple measures matter.* Retrieved from http://www.gallup.com/services/191261/assessment-work-students-multiple-measures-matter.aspx

Ginsberg, M., & Wlodkowski, R. (2004). *Creating highly motivating classrooms.* San Francisco, CA: Jossey-Bass.

Gladwell, M. (2008). *Outliers: The story of success.* New York: Little, Brown, and Company.

Good, T. L. (1987). Two decades of research on teacher expectations: Findings and future directions. *Journal of Teacher Education, 38*(4), 32–47.

Grossman, P. (1990). *The making of a teacher.* New York, NY: Teachers College Press.

Harper, B., & Milman, N. B. (2016). One-to-one technology in K–12 classrooms: A review of the literature from 2004 through 2014. *Journal of Research on Technology in Education, 48*(2), 129–142.

Hattie, J. (2009). *Visible learning: A synthesis of over 800 meta-analyses relating to achievement.* New York, NY: Routledge.

Hattie, J. (2012). *Visible learning for teachers: Maximizing impact on learning.* New York: Routledge.

Hattie, J. (2015). The applicability of visible learning to higher education. *Scholarship of Teaching and Learning in Psychology, 1*(1), 79–91.

Hattie, J., & Timperley, H. (2007). The power of feedback. *Review of Educational Research, 77*(1), 81–112.

Hess, R. S., & Copeland, E. P. (2001). Students' stress, coping strategies, and school completion: A longitudinal perspective. *School Psychology Quarterly, 16,* 389–405.

Israel, E. (2002). Examining multiple perspectives in literature. In J. Holden & J. S. Schmit (Eds.), *Inquiry and the literary text: Constructing discussions in the English classroom* (pp. 90–103). Urbana, IL: NCTE.

Ivey, G., & Broaddus, K. (2001). "Just plain reading": A survey of what makes students want to read in middle school classrooms. *Reading Research Quarterly, 36,* 350–377.

Jacobs, V. R., Lamb, L. C., & Philipp, R. A. (2010). Professional noticing of children's mathematical thinking. *Journal for Research in Mathematics Education, 41*(2), 169–202.

Kapur, M. (2008). Productive failure. *Cognition and Instruction, 26*(3), 379–424.

Kapur, M. (2014). Failure can be productive for teaching children maths. *The Conversation*. Retrieved from http://theconversation.com/failure-can-be-productive-for-teaching-children-maths-22418

King, J. B., Jr. (2017, January 17). A dispatch from the outgoing U.S. education secretary: America has the right to a great public education. *Education Week, 36*(18), 28.

Klem, A. M., & Connell, J. P. (2004). Relationships matter: Linking teacher support to student engagement and achievement. *Journal of School Health, 74,* 262–273.

Klingner, J. K., & Vaughn, S. (1999). Promoting reading comprehension, content learning, and English acquisition through Collaborative Strategic Reading (CSR). *The Reading Teacher, 52*(7), 738–747.

Knight, J. (2016). *Better conversations: Coaching ourselves and each other to be more credible, caring, and connected.* Thousand Oaks, CA: Corwin.

LaBerge, D., & Samuels, S. J. (1974). Toward a theory of automatic information process in reading. *Cognitive Psychology, 6,* 293–323.

Lewis, A., Huebner, E. S., Malone, P., & Valois, R. F. (2011). Life satisfaction and student engagement in adolescence. *Journal of Youth and Adolescence, 40,* 249–262.

Los Angeles County Office of Education. (2002). *Teacher expectations and student achievement coordinator manual.* Downey, CA: Author.

Mason, J. M., Stahl, S. A., Au, K. H., & Herman, P. A. (2003). Reading: Children's developing knowledge of words. In J. Flood, D. Lapp, J. R. Squire, & J. M. Jensen (Eds.), *Handbook of research on teaching the English language arts* (2nd ed., pp. 914–930). Mahwah, NJ: Erlbaum.

McKown, C., & Weinstein, R. S. (2008). Teacher expectations, classroom context, and the achievement gap. *Journal of School Psychology, 46*(3), 235–261.

Meyerson, D., Weick, K. E., & Kramer, R. M. (1996). Swift trust and temporary groups. In R. Kramer & T. Tyler (Eds.), *Trust in organizations: Frontiers of theory and research* (pp. 166–195). Thousand Oaks, CA: SAGE.

Midgley, C., Kaplan, A., & Middleton, M. J. (2001). Performance-approach goals: Good for what, for whom, under what circumstances, and at what cost? *Journal of Educational Psychology, 93*(1), 77–86.

Miller, A. (1949). *Death of a salesman.* New York, NY: Viking Penguin.

Nathan, M. J., & Petrosino, A. (2003). Expert blind spot among preservice teachers. *American Educational Research Journal, 40*(4), 905–928.

National Governors Association Center for Best Practices and Council of Chief State School Officers. (2010). *Common core state standards.* Washington, DC: Author.

National Research Council and Institute of Medicine. (2004). *Engaging schools: Fostering high school students' motivation to learn.* Washington, DC: National Academies Press.

Newmann, F., Wehlage, G. G., & Lamborn, S. D. (1992). The significance and sources of student engagement. In F. Newmann (Ed.), *Student engagement and achievement in American secondary schools* (pp. 11–39). New York, NY: Teachers College Press.

Palincsar, A. S., & Brown, A. (1984). Reciprocal teaching of comprehension-fostering and comprehension-monitoring activities. *Cognition and Instruction, 1*(2), 117–175.

Parker, P. D., Jerrim, J., Schoon, I., & Marsh, H. W. (2016). A multi-nation study of socioeconomic inequality in expectations for progression to higher education. *American Educational Research Journal, 53*(1), 6–32.

Penn, H. (2008). *Understanding early childhood: Issues and controversies* (2nd ed.). New York, NY: Open University Press.

Pilgreen, J. L. (2000). *The SSR handbook: How to organize and manage a sustained silent reading program.* Portsmouth, NH: Boynton/Cook.

Pratt, S. M., & Urbanowski, M. (2015). Teaching early readers to self-monitor and self-correct. *The Reading Teacher, 69*(5), 559–567.

Purkey, W. W. (1991). *What is invitational education and how does it work?* Paper presented at the 9th annual California State Conference on Self-Esteem, Santa Clara, CA.

Purkey, W. W., & Novak, J. M. (1996). *Inviting school success: A self-concept approach to teaching, learning, and democratic practice* (3rd ed.). Belmont, CA: Wadsworth.

Quaglia, R. (2016). *Principal voice: Listen, learn, lead.* Thousand Oaks, CA: Corwin.

Quaglia, R., & Corso, M. (2014). *Student voice: The instrument of change.* Thousand Oaks, CA: Corwin.

Quaglia, R., Corso, M., Fox, K., & Dykes, G. (2017). *Aspire high: Imagining tomorrow's school today.* Thousand Oaks, CA: Corwin.

Quaglia Institute for School Voice and Aspirations. (2016). *School voice report 2016.* Retrieved from http://quagliainstitute.org/dmsView/School_Voice_Report_2016

Quaglia, R., & Lande, L. (2017). *Teacher voice: Amplifying success.* Thousand Oaks, CA: Corwin.

Ryan, A. M., Pintrich, P. R., & Midgley, C. (2001). Avoiding seeking help in the classroom: Who and why? *Educational Psychology Review, 13*, 93–114.

Samuels, S. J. (1979). The method of repeated reading. *The Reading Teacher, 32*(4), 403–408.

Sapon-Shevin, M. (2010). *Because we can change the world: A practical guide to building cooperative, inclusive classroom communities* (2nd ed.). Thousand Oaks, CA: Corwin.

Schneider, S. K., O'Donnell, L., Stueve, A., & Coulter, R. W. S. (2012). Cyberbullying, school bullying, and psychological distress: A regional census of high school students. *American Journal of Public Health, 102*, 171–177.

Shulman, L. S. (1987). Knowledge and teaching: Foundations of the new reform. *Harvard Educational Review, 57*(1), 1–22.

Simmons, J. (2003). Responders are taught, not born. *Journal of Adolescent and Adult Literacy, 46,* 684–693.

Skinner, E. A., Pitzer, J. R., & Steele, J. S. (2016). Can student engagement serve as a motivational resource for academic coping, persistence, and learning during late elementary and early middle school? *Developmental Psychology, 52*(12), 2099–2117.

Smith, T. W., Baker, W. K., Hattie, J. A. C., & Bond, L. (2008). A validity study of the certification system of the National Board for Professional Teaching Standards. In L. Ingvarson & J. A. C. Hattie (Eds.), *Assessing teachers for professional certification: The first decade of the National Board for Professional Teaching Standards* (pp. 345–380). Advances in Program Evaluation Series #11. Oxford: Elsevier.

Smothers, E. F. (2003). *The hard-times jar.* New York, NY: Farrar, Straus, and Giroux.

Stanovich, K. E. (1986). Matthew effects in reading: Some consequences of individual differences in the acquisition of literacy. *Reading Research Quarterly, 22,* 360–407.

Tough, P. (2012). *How children succeed: Grit, curiosity, and the hidden power of character.* New York, NY: Houghton Mifflin Harcourt.

Vygotsky, L. S. (1978). *Mind in society* (Trans. M. Cole). Cambridge, MA: Harvard University Press.

Wang, M. T., Willett, J. B., & Eccles, J. S. (2011). The assessment of school engagement: Examining dimensionality and measurement invariance across gender and race/ethnicity. *Journal of School Psychology, 49,* 465–480.

Wexler, B. E., Iseli, M., Leon, S., Zaggle, W., Rush, C., Goodman, A., . . . Bo, E. (2016). Cognitive priming and cognitive training: Immediate and far transfer to academic skills in children. *Scientific Reports, 6.* doi:10.1038/srep32859

Wiggins, G. (2012). Seven keys to effective feedback. *Educational Leadership, 70*(1), 10–16.

Wiggins, G., & McTighe, J. (2011). The understanding by design guide to creating high-quality units. Alexandria, VA: ASCD.

Willems, M. (2014). *Waiting is not easy.* New York, NY: Disney-Hyperion.

Index

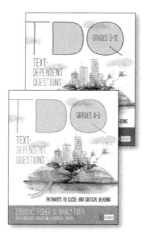

CORWIN

A SAGE Publishing Company

Helping educators make the greatest impact

CORWIN HAS ONE MISSION: to enhance education through intentional professional learning.

We build long-term relationships with our authors, educators, clients, and associations who partner with us to develop and continuously improve the best evidence-based practices that establish and support lifelong learning.

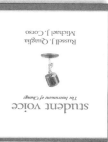
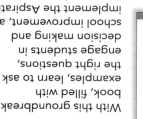
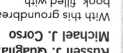